THE SAGA OF MANCHESTER LINERS

by

Robert B. Stoker

KINGLISH LIMITED,
DOUGLAS, ISLE OF MAN

ISBN 0 9507480 2 1

Printed by Print Centres Ltd., Spring Valley Industrial Estate,
Braddan, Isle of Man

About the author

ROBERT BURDON STOKER is the third generation of his family to have taken the helm of Manchester Liners.

His grandfather, also Robert Burdon Stoker, the company's first managing director and subsequently chairman, was succeeded by his son, Kenneth, father of the author.

Mr. Stoker served Manchester Liners for 47 years, until retiring in 1979 — when he was described by Commodore Alan Cookson as "Mr. Manchester Liners".

An author, poet, painter and historian as well as businessman, Mr. Stoker joined the company in the Dock Office at the age of 18 in 1932. His job, making returns, was speeded by his ability to write at the same time with both hands!

He was appointed executive director in 1951, succeeded his father as Managing Director in 1965 and as Chairman in 1968.

During the 1939-45 war he was Deputy Ministry of War Transport Representative at the Convoy Anchorage, Gourock, Scotland, and also in the Mediterranean, where his unconventional methods and achievements earned him a reputation as the "uncrowned King of Sicily".

In this story Mr. Stoker paints a vivid — and often humourous — picture of the years during which Manchester Liners played a major role in Manchester's development from an inland city to a port with world-wide interests.

Under his leadership in the post-war years Manchester Liners achieved many "firsts" — first British company into the Great Lakes, first ship into the St. Lawrence Seaway, the first British deep-sea container service, the first shipping company to gain the Queen's Export Award.

Mr. R. B. Stoker, grandson of the first Managing Director and Chairman of Manchester Liners

Numerous directorships included Furness, Withy and Company, Barclays Bank and British Engine Insurance, of which he was chairman. He was President of Manchester Chamber of Commerce, founded the Manchester Junior Chamber, has been President or Chairman of numerous bodies such as the Institute of Shipping and Forwarding Agents concerned with shipping, business and welfare.

He holds an honorary MA degree granted by Manchester University and was awarded the Queen's Jubilee Medal in 1977.

In addition to "The Saga of Manchester Liners" Mr. Stoker has had published "The Legacy of Arthur's Chester", and "Cheshire's Greatest Battle".

He lives in Wilmslow, Cheshire.

Introduction

THE "Saga of Manchester Liners" is the story of the company from 1898 to 1984, written by Mr. Stoker in three stages, now brought within the covers of one volume. All were originally published in **Sea Breezes**.

The first account "50 Years on the Western Ocean" took the story to 1948, the second "60 Years on the Western Ocean", added a further decade.

The third account takes in the 25 years to 1984, a quarter century packed with some of the most exciting and far-reaching developments in world shipping.

This was a period which saw Manchester Liners blazing a trail in shipping history by taking the lead in Britain in the move from conventional to containerised services, operating the country's first purpose-built fully-cellular container vessel the ***Manchester Challenge*** from Manchester to Montreal in November 1968.

Inevitably, the "container revolution" brought great changes, as traumatic in its effect as the change from sail to steam.

The 1970s and early '80s saw a cargo "Battle of the Atlantic" so ferocious that companies went out of existence, only the strongest and most determined surviving.

The design of vessels leapt ahead in sophistication, their size and container capacity rose dramatically, the number of ships operated decreased, ports had to adapt, if possible, to change. Traditional markets were developed in new ways, fresh markets were created.

Among the casualties in the 1980s: the upper reaches of the Manchester Ship Canal. Salford Docks and the Manchester Ship Canal, opened in 1894 by Queen Victoria, played a vital part in the growth and development of the region for 100 years. But, overtaken by events, the canal's upper reaches were practically bereft of shipping by 1984.

In April of that year the Manchester Ship Canal Company announced its intention to seek the closure of the canal to navigation, from Runcorn to Manchester, by early 1987.

At the time of writing (1985) the closure option was being held in abeyance pending investigations into the feasibility of saving the upper reaches for continued commercial use or new leisure uses.

A development plan published in March 1985 envisaged a mixture of residential, commercial, leisure and recreation schemes, taking their character from the waterside setting.

THE MEN BEHIND THE SHIPS

MANY men who made their mark in shipping hail from the North East of England. The first Mr. R. B. Stoker, destined to set Manchester Liners on course, was born there in 1859.

In 1855, James Knott, later Sir James, was born in Northumberland. He founded the Prince Line, whose fortunes were to intertwine in 1968 with Manchester Liners through the Manchester Prince Line, a move which took Manchester Liners into the Mediterranean.

Both companies are members of Furness, Withy (Shipping) Ltd., part of the Furness, Withy Group.

At the age of 17, the first Mr. Stoker, as was the custom in those days — and possibly still is in Norway — was given his first ship, a 500-ton coaster, by his father.

He also entered a Liverpool sailing ship firm which changed into a steam shipping company, of which he became manager. Significantly, this company was very much involved in the American and Canadian trades, a fact which considerably influenced the later development of Manchester Liners.

By the time Mr. Stoker was 23 his name was well-known in shipping circles and Christopher Furness, later Sir Christopher, invited him in 1882 to become one of his aides. Furness was 30 years of age.

Having spent three months in West Hartlepool, Mr. Stoker opened an office in Newcastle upon Tyne for the start of the Furness Line to North America. The American railways were expanding and there were westbound cargoes of pig and bar iron from the Tees, Tyne, Stockholm and Gothenburg, plus coal from the Tyne and South Wales. Homeward cargo included grain, flour, apples and live cattle.

Within two years the Furness Line was operating 10 ships: the ***New York City, Boston City, Durham City, Newcastle City, Wetherby, Gothenburg City, Stockholm City, Ripon City, Lincoln City*** and ***Calcutta City***. Within four years three more vessels had been added, the ***Washington City, Ulunda*** and ***Damara***, on charter.

With an established and profitable line behind him, Christopher Furness was able to buy a controlling interest in shipbuilders Edward Withy and Company, of West Hartlepool.

In 1890 R. B. Stoker was asked to go to London to open an office to take over operations there, which had been looked after by Adamson and Ronaldson. By this time he also owned a 3,500-ton tramp steamer named the ***Sydenham*** and later the steamer ***Knutsford***.

In 1891 Furness, Withy and Company was formed with Christopher Furness as chairman, R. B. Stoker as ship director, Edward Withy and R. W. Vick as shipyard representatives, plus Thomas King and G. L. Wooley.

Christopher Furness's godson, Frederick Lewis (later Sir Frederick) was sent to the London office for training as a junior. He had much ability and business acumen, as was demonstrated during an important meeting in London when Christopher Furness was asked the state of Furness, Withy's finances.

Furness called in young Lewis and asked, "Freddy, what is our bank balance?"

"£10,000, sir", was the prompt reply. That was the figure in the red. The response was in keeping with the spirit of shipowning at the time.

The novel "Grand Hotel, Babylon" by Arnold Bennett is said to be based on an apocryphal story told about Sir Christopher Furness. On being cheeked by the head porter at the Grand Hotel, Harrogate, Sir Christopher is reputed to have bought the hotel and sacked the porter. Certainly R. B. Stoker used to stay at the hotel on favourable terms.

In 1896 he went to New York to buy the Philadelphia Trans-Atlantic Line, returning after six months. During this period, events had been moving at Manchester where, led by Daniel Adamson, a group of businessmen had been building the 35-mile long Manchester Ship Canal, turning the inland city into a major port. It was officially opened to traffic on January 1, 1894, an opening ceremony being performed later, on May 21, by Queen Victoria, who sailed through the waterway in the Royal Yacht ***Enchantress***.

Manchester decided it would have to operate ships of its own. For two years Furness, Withy and Company had sent a few ships in from Canada and Sir Christopher agreed to take up £50,000-worth of ordinary shares in a new local company if Manchester interests could raise £200,000.

Two directors of the Manchester Ship Canal Company, Sir Bosdin Leech and Alderman Southern, visited Canada, receiving promises of a subsidy of £8,000 a year from the Canadian Government and support from big shippers, including the Canadian Ministry of Agriculture, the Canadian Pacific Railway and a Mr. Swift, of Chicago.

On May 5, 1898 the prospectus of Manchester Liners Ltd. was announced, with a total issuable capital of £1mn. The directors were Sir Christopher Furness, as chairman; Mr. C. Schiff, who had big South American interests; Alderman Southern and Sir Edward Jenkinson, KCB, directors of the Manchester Ship Canal Company; and Sir Richard Mottram, of Salford.

Mr. R. B. Stoker resigned from the board of Furness, Withy and Co. Ltd. to become the first managing director of Manchester Liners Ltd.

A contemporary article in **Syren and Shipping** said that Mr. Stoker had "made two hits and there is every reason to believe that he will make a third". The article went on to say that Mr. Stoker had seen great promise for the future of Manchester shipowning and had been a pioneer of overseas trade from "cottonopolis".

"With a shrewd man of business, an able administrator at the head of affairs and the capital of Lancashire behind it, Manchester Liners Ltd. should flourish exceedingly", concluded the article.

In those days owners had to rely on ships' masters to perform many tasks later carried out by agents. Furness was keen to meet and assess potential appointees to Manchester Liners, frequently doing so at West Hartlepool, the town for which he had just proudly become Member of Parliament.

A master seeking a job with Manchester Liners arrived at the West Hartlepool office to be asked by Furness: "Well, captain, what do you think of West Hartlepool?"

An honest — but ex-prospective — ML master replied: "Well, sir, I think it is a bit of a dump!"

In 1900 Sir Christopher, with his North East Line, his London-USA Line, and a big stake in Manchester Liners, also decided to go into insurance. With Mr. Stoker and Mr. Guthe, head of the West Hartlepool Steam Navigation Company, he founded the Economic Insurance Company, which remained part of the Furness empire until it was sold in the 1970s.

In 1912, on the death of Lord Furness, as he had become, Mr. Stoker was elected chairman of Manchester Liners, remaining in office until he died in 1919. He lived in Knutsford — and served as Member of Parliament for the Rusholme Division of Manchester.

Mr. Stoker was succeeded in the chair by Sir Frederick Lewis (later Lord Essendon), who died in 1944, being succeeded by Mr. Ernest (later Sir Ernest) Murrant.

It was in 1919 that Mr. Kenneth Stoker, son of R. B. Stoker, became a director of Manchester Liners. He was appointed managing director in 1932,

Sir Ernest Murrant, KCMG, MBE, Chairman of Manchester Liners, 1944-1959

This cartoon "The Great Transportation Scene" was published in "Syren and Shipping" in 1899. It shows Sir Christopher Furness, later Viscount Furness (centre front) and R. B. Stoker, first managing director of Manchester Liners (third from right, front). A framed version is in the possession of the author

succeeding Mr. F. E. Vaughan, and became chairman in 1959.

Mr. Kenneth Stoker retired in June 1968 at the age of 82 after 49 years as a director and became the company's first honorary president. Still fit and active — he was a notable golfer and skier — he attended at Manchester Liners House in 1975 to present his chairman son with a gold 40-plus years' long service wristlet watch. He remained honorary president until his death in October 1979 at the age of 93.

On the retirement of Mr. Stoker, Mr. W. A. L. (Tony) Roberts became chairman, continuing as managing director.

Mr. Roberts, son of Manchester Ship Canal chairman Sir Leslie Roberts CBE, joined Manchester Liners in January 1948 as a management trainee after service as a company commanding officer in the Grenadier Guards. He started in the dock office and moved on to serve in all the company's departments as well as studying the company's business during two years in Canada, including travelling as a salesman.

In April 1960 he was appointed a director with particular responsibilities for North Atlantic freight, as deputy managing director in 1965 and as managing director in January 1968.

In the 1960s development of the container concept was his special responsibility. Mr. Roberts retired in 1984.

At the time of Mr. Stoker's retirement, Sir Errington Keville, a national shipping figure, also retired, being succeeded as chairman of Furness, Withy and Co. Ltd. by Mr. James A. MacConochie, who joined the Manchester Liners board.

* * *

IN THE BEGINNING

THE story has often been told how the Manchester Ship Canal was built but seldom how the ships came to it. A port, however well equipped, is useless without ships and some superintendents are alleged to have sneered at the "dirty ditch" which they reckoned was only safe for vessels up to 370 ft. in length and was not seriously to be regarded as suitable for modern ocean-going ships.

The city of Manchester was ill-equipped for dealing with overseas trade, the banks were unused to bills of lading, the produce market was not organised and one cargo of fruit had to be railed to London to be sold. Some London and Newcastle owners sent in medium-sized vessels but the port was only doing a fraction of its potential business.

Manchester decided that it would have to operate ships of its own and Manchester Liners was formed, the prospectus being issued on May 5, 1898.

Two vessels were purchased from Elder Dempster and Co. Ltd., the ***Queensmore*** and ***Parkmore***, which had previously been owned by the Johnston Line. Both these vessels were well-known in the Canadian trade, and at the time were running on Elder Dempster Line's service from Avonmouth; also two additional ships were chartered, the ***Cynthiana*** and the ***Straits of Menai***. The ***Queensmore***, 360 ft. long and of 3,878 tons gross, set a record as being the largest ship to reach the port from Canada; her name was changed to ***Manchester Enterprise***, while the ***Parkmore*** became ***Manchester Trader***. These vessels were equipped for carrying cattle, the ***Queensmore*** bringing 450 head.

Great enthusiasm had been aroused in Canada by the new Manchester grain

An early cartoon in which the first Robert B. Stoker was shown hauling ships along the Manchester Ship Canal. The title: "A Modern Gulliver"

elevator, described as the "finest on the planet" by the people of Manchester in a cable to Chicago. Those were great days for Manchester. Her people were proud of their city, their new Ship Canal, and their achievements, and they let the world know it. The ***Parkmore*** (Capt. W. J. Parry) was the first vessel to bring grain in bulk to this elevator which has since helped to bring so much prosperity to the milling trade of Manchester.

Furness, Withy and Company opened a new office in Montreal and became the new line's Montreal agents. Within a month of its establishment Mr. George Robertson, three times mayor of Saint John, N.B., was speaking at the Manchester town hall on the possibilities of trade between the two cities. Manchester Liners decided to make Saint John their terminal winter port.

In September 1898, Furness, Withy bought the business of Mr. S. Schofield, who continued as their manager to look after the new line; this materially helped to consolidate Saint John's position as a winter port, since the greater part of the goods for Canada were then going through American ports. On the return journey the new line called at Halifax for lumber. Thus was started an unbroken link of half-a-century between Manchester and these three Canadian cities.

Within a few months the new company was also loading ships for New Orleans and Galveston, to return with cotton. That first season the company handled 13 ships from Galveston, Brunswick and New Orleans, carrying 62,258 bales of cotton; this service was later continued as a joint one with Frederick Leyland and Co. Ltd. It was also announced that a service would be commenced to Boston with the ***Gloriana, Italiana*** and ***Cynthiana***.

At the end of October 1898, the ***Manchester City*** was launched, by Sir Raylton Dixon & Co. Ltd., at Middlesbrough, and at once became famous as the largest vessel built on the Tees with an overall length of 461 ft., deadweight capacity of 8,600 tons, refrigerated space, accommodation for 700 cattle and a speed of 12½ to 13 knots. "Famous at Saint John, N.B., as the greatest vessel ever seen there; famous at Liverpool as a ship built to do that which has often been declared by Liverpool shipowners to be impossible for any vessel of her size; and famous in Manchester as the first ship built for Manchester Liners Ltd., and the biggest steamer by 1,000 tons or more that ever attempted to navigate the Ship Canal". ("Manchester Guardian").

The same paper (16.1.99) tells the saga of this first trip up the canal. How "there were many shakings of the head, not in Liverpool only, over the audacity of the attempt". How for the first half-mile up the "ditch" the idle spectators were rather worried but Pilot George Cartwright and Capt. Forrest passed other vessels and brought her through the locks without scratching the paint. That night she stopped at Irlam to give the pilots, officers and engineers a well earned rest — the pilots "looking as if they had not been in bed for a week, after they have finished the day's work, for their eyes are bleared with exhaustion".

Next day she discharged 450 head of cattle and 150 sheep at Mode Wheel lairages and reached Manchester, with the port decorated, to await a reception from the Lord Mayor. It was a great day for Manchester: the bogey that only medium-sized ships could navigate the canal was exorcised and the port was now able to attract the largest cargo ships then afloat.

The representatives of the Southern Dominions wired to their homelands that modern ships able to reach Australia could now berth at Manchester. Mr. Marshall Stevens, who had taken over Trafford Park Estate, made a jubilant speech.

On her first outward trip from Manchester the ***City***, in March 1899, reached Halifax in 9 days 16 hours, beating the mail boat which left the Mersey 12 hours ahead of her. And Manchester Liners followed up by launching in April 1899, the ***Manchester Port***, of 467 ft. overall, built by Palmers at Jarrow. In May the ***Manchester Importer*** and in July a sister-ship, the ***Manchester Shipper***, both products of Irvine's Shipbuilding Company, West Hartlepool, were launched.

In June 1899, the Furness, Withy shipyard at West Hartlepool launched the ***Manchester Corporation***, while her sister the ***Manchester Commerce***, was under construction, and in July the ***Manchester Merchant*** was launched at Irvine's. All of these vessels carried a few passengers in comfortable quarters and over the years the standard of accommodation improved until many people travelled only in these cargo liners.

Meantime the war in South Africa speeded up and the new ***Manchester Port*** (Capt. M'Lennan), after beating the mail steamer on her maiden voyage, was taken by the Government to embark the 1st Royal Dragoons. It is on record that their colonel wired to the honorary colonel, the Emperor Wilhelm of Germany, "I have the honour to announce that your Majesty's British Regiment of Royal Dragoons will leave Tilbury Dock next Sunday on board the ship ***Manchester Port*** for South Africa", to which the Kaiser replied: "I thank you for your telegram. Convey my farewell to the Regiment. May you all come back uninjured and well".

"The Times" (30.10.99) reported "This message gave the liveliest satisfaction to the troops". The ***Manchester Port*** also took out the first unaccompanied shipment of wireless telegraphy instruments which had never before been used in warfare and which it was confidently predicted by the experts of Signor Marconi would supercede the signalling lamp!

In the Western Ocean in December 1898, the homeward bound ***Manchester Enterprise*** (Capt. Wright) was towed into Queenstown by the ***Cephalonia*** as a result of heavy weather damage. On November 15, 1899, she foundered during a gale; fortunately the crew were rescued by the ***Lakonia*** (Capt. M'Neill) of the Donaldson Line. The ***Enterprise*** was quite a good ship except that she "just leaked", and one witness at the enquiry suggested that she rolled in dry dock! The "Manchester Guardian", after commenting on her two previous ownerships, added (19.1.1900) "certainly the ships the Manchester Liners have built for themselves are very unlike her".

The ***Trader***, built in 1890, was also a remarkable ship in that she was able to travel quicker going astern in a head wind than ahead with her engines. On two voyages she reached Queenstown 10 days after leaving the Mersey!

The new ***Manchester Corporation*** took 500 troops and 400 horses to South Africa, and so satisfied were the authorities with the care given to the animals that they arranged a second voyage, while the ***Manchester City*** brought mules from New Orleans. The new ***Manchester Merchant*** embarked West Country yeomanry and the owners were also complimented by the colonel in a special message. The ***Port***, after a second trip, then went on to Australia to bring Imperial troops to South Africa. The ***Port*** was sold to R. P. Houston and Company, becoming the ***Hydaspes***, and replaced.

Meanwhile the Western Ocean service was maintained. In other St. Lawrence ports, Chicoutimi, Quebec, Rimouski and Charlottetown, the "M.L." flag became known.

Delivered in 1918, the "Manchester Brigade" was an early Second World War casualty. She was torpedoed and sunk in September 1940

In 1900 the trade of the port had increased so rapidly that the Ship Canal Company sought compulsory powers to obtain land for No. 9 dock; the evidence of Manchester Liners, who had brought in 47 ships in nine months, was a big factor in the House of Lords committee assenting to this. Assisted by Mr. R. Dawson Harling, who had opened a Canadian office for the Ship Canal Company, new business was created as this additional channel for trade became recognised.

The Manchester Wholesale Provision Trade Association, which had "hailed with joy" the ***Manchester City***, saw their business doubled in a year and enthusiastically supported the new service which Manchester Liners opened to Philadelphia in 1901, regarded as "of great benefit to the district". The line was run jointly with R. W. Leyland and Company, of Liverpool, and the first sailings were the ***Manchester Corporation*** and Leyland's ***Planet Neptune*** to the piers of the Reading Railroad.

By 1902 the Commercial Fruit Rooms in Manchester, opened a few years before, were doing a large trade in apples from Halifax. Created by the new service, this trade has been of great benefit to Nova Scotia for nearly half a century.

Not many new and struggling companies lose, in peace time, three ships in nearly as many years. Such, however, was the case with Manchester Liners Ltd., for on January 14, 1903, the new ***Manchester Merchant*** caught fire when laden with a full cargo of cotton from New Orleans to Manchester and was beached in Dingle Bay; and on April 26 the new ***Market*** outward bound from Manchester to Philadelphia, hit the Tuskar Rock in fog.

The longer the task of writing the history of a company is put off, the greater the work of the historian, who will find that records get destroyed, the older generation passes on, memories fade, and facts become legends. The legend in this case is that the master of the ***Market*** came off the bridge to shut a door when he thought he heard banging and found too late that the noise was not caused by a banging door!

In 1904 the fleet consisted of 14 ships of 94,657 tons deadweight and 61,696 gross, as follows:—

	Gross
Manchester City (Capt. M. Forest)	5,833
Manchester Corporation (Capt. P. J. Heath)	5,473
Manchester Commerce (Capt. W. P. Couch)	5,363
Manchester Engineer (Capt. A. T. Haworth)	4,302
Manchester Inventor (Capt. C. Payne)	4,262
Manchester Spinner (Capt. F. Mann)	4,226
Manchester Miller (Capt. E. W. C. Beggs)	4,234
Manchester Merchant (Capt. J. R. Foale)	4,151
Manchester Port (Capt. J. Y. Acraman)	4,092
Manchester Mariner (Capt. P. Linton)	4,106
Manchester Importer (Capt. W. J. Parry)	4,208
Manchester Shipper (Capt. L. Morton)	4,038
Manchester Exchange (Capt. H. Varwell)	4,091
Manchester Trader (Capt. G. F. Fisher)	3,317

In the same year a monthly service to the River Plate was started and in 1906 this service combined with F. Leyland and Company to give a fortnightly sailing, every other ship loading at Glasgow. Owing, however, to lack of support from Manchester merchants, it was suspended in 1908, but the ***City*** continued to run between the River Plate and other British ports. The vessel was then fully insulated and, chartered by the Anglo-Argentine Shipping Company, created a further record by carrying the largest consignment of frozen and chilled meat up to that time.

The years from 1902 till 1912 were years of anxiety and cut-throat competition which reduced freights to a low level, while shippers in Manchester who had benefited so greatly were withholding their support. As their three ships in other trades paid twice as well as those serving Manchester there was a constant suggestion that the company should cease being a "philanthropic institution" and give up its services to Manchester in which the

Third ship to bear the name "Manchester Commerce" dated from 1925 and became a war loss off West Africa in July 1943

ships had failed to earn depreciation for some years.

For six years before the tide showed signs of turning the company struggled to continue its regular services to its home port. Ordinary shareholders received no dividend between 1903 and 1912, and by 1911 the preference dividends were five and a half years in arrears. One shareholder rather pathetically hoped that: "We will soon get a dividend because soon we shall be where dividends are of no use and are not wanted".

One annual meeting was held at noon on a Saturday at which the chairman was unable to attend and at which it was hoped that none of the aggreived shareholders would attend — this was a very forlorn hope.

During this period the ***Manchester Corporation*** created the record of being the only ship successfully to "whitewash" the Ship Canal! In 1908 a shipment of lard in bulk was being discharged at night into barges alongside and "by some inexplicable mischance was pumped into the Salford Docks".

It is believed that next morning when the engineer responsible saw the Ship Canal white as far as the eye could see, he did not wait to be sacked, but just packed his bags. The lard, we understand, was skimmed off the top, refined and subsequently consumed.

In 1911 a working arrangement was made with three Canadian Great Lakes steamship companies, the Northern Steamship Company, the Island Transportation Company, and the Richelieu & Ontario Company, whereby a through service was given from Duluth and Port Arthur by water to Montreal, for transhipment to Manchester. Furness, Withy and Company, Montreal, became linked with the board of the Northern Steamship Company. This gave a great impetus to trade on Canada's inland waterways.

By 1913, however, the Port of Manchester had become the fourth port of the Kingdom and Manchester Liners handled 524,000 tons of cargo. The ***Manchester Trader*** had been sold and two new vessels, the ***Manchester Citizen*** and the ***Manchester Civilian***, had been added to the fleet, which had risen to 102,156 tons deadweight comprising:—

	D.W.
Manchester City (refrigerated)	9,117
Manchester Commerce	7,848
Manchester Corporation	7,848
Manchester Citizen	7,450
Manchester Engineer	7,200
Manchester Inventor	7,170
Manchester Spinner	7,158
Manchester Miller	7,153
Manchester Merchant	6,982
Manchester Importer	6,966
Manchester Shipper	6,951
Manchester Port	6,906
Manchester Mariner	6,838
Manchester Exchange	6,569

On the death of Lord Furness, Mr. R. B. Stoker, who had been managing director from the inception of the company, was elected chairman.

FIRST WORLD WAR

THEN came the First World War and Manchester's ships and Manchester's seamen played their part in the long, grim struggle.

Two days after the outbreak of war the ***Manchester Engineer*** (Capt. R. Smith) was requisitioned as a transport, hastened to Southampton and delivered her first load of men and stores in France on August 21, 1914. Through the days of the retreat to Mons and until June, 1915, she was carrying on this essential service. She caught fire in March, 1915, but was repaired. Then on her third voyage home from the U.S.A. with supplies she was torpedoed off Waterford on March 27, 1916.

The ***Manchester Importer*** was also requisitioned the same day and landed her first cargo of "Old Contemptibles" to the Western Front at Havre on August 17, 1914. Khaki was not available, and troops went to France in their scarlet jackets and busbies! She continued to carry men, guns and horses across the Channel without mishap until May 20, 1918, when she was torpedoed, but, under the command of Capt. P. Linton, managed to reach Southampton safely.

The ***Manchester Citizen,*** which sailed soon after war broke out, managed to evade the raider ***Kaiser Wilhelm der Grosse.***

On the night of October 26/27, 1914, the four masted steamer ***Manchester Commerce,*** outward bound, was sunk by a mine off Tory Island, being the first merchant ship to be mined. One lifeboat was launched and the master, Capt. Payne, with other members of the crew were preparing another for launching when the steamer sank, within seven minutes of striking the mine. Those left on board had to jump into an extremely rough sea; some managed to swim to the first lifeboat, but the captain and 13 others were drowned.

The first intimation of this loss was apparently when the Fleetwood trawler ***City of London*** put into Carnlough Bay, Co. Antrim, and reported her rescue of 30 survivors. The disaster occurred on on of the routes fixed by the Admiralty which had been communicated by secret instructions to shipmasters and shipowners a very short time previously. The speed and facility with which the route was mined proved that the German Secret Service agents had discovered the Admiralty's instructions and had been instrumental in the despatch of a ship wearing neutral colours to lay the minefield.

A ship flying the Swedish flag had been observed in the mine area, behaving suspiciously. It subsequently transpired that the vessel was the former 17-knot Norddeutscher Lloyd liner ***Berlin,*** which, being in home waters at the outbreak of war, had been fitted out as a mine layer. The next day a battleship was sunk in the same minefield. A new, and lurking danger lay in wait for ships.

At the other end of the world Von Spee's squadron was sweeping the South Pacific and Admiral Sturdee's two battle-cruisers ***Invincible*** and ***Inflexible*** were despatched to the Falkland Islands. There, as they were coaling from the ***Manchester Civilian*** (Capt. G. Spencer), the Germans appeared. Casting off at once the battle-cruisers engaged Von Spee and the South Atlantic was freed from the menace of the raiders.

The ***Civilian*** continued on Admiralty work through 1915. It is reported that when years later Admiral Sturdee came round the Manchester Docks he saluted the ***Manchester Civilian,*** which had taken an honourable and essential part in this campaign. On release from the Admiralty she carried stores from Canada to Dunkirk.

At the outbreak of war the Austrian Lloyd had a vessel on the stocks; this 11-knot ship was taken over, completed by the Liners and named ***Manchester Hero.*** Under the command of Capt. Perry, she was pursued and shelled by a submarine off the West Coast of Ireland but escaped through volunteers in the stokehold whipping her up to a speed believed to be 16 knots, from which effort, it is said, she never fully recovered.

Even in war the natural hazards of the sea are still present, and on November 12, 1915, the ***Manchester Merchant*** (Capt. E. W. C. Beggs and Chief Officer (later Capt) H. Brown) *en route* from Canada, saved 15 men from the Brazilian barque ***Storeng*** foundering in a gale. This gallant feat was recognised by a reception from the Lord Mayor of Manchester, also by the Liverpool Shipwreck and Humane Society.

More than 18 months of war and only one casualty — would our luck hold? It did not.

On March 27, 1916 the ***Manchester Engineer*** (Capt. R. Smith) was sunk. The following year, the ***Manchester Inventor*** (Capt. H. Williams) which since the beginning of the war had been bringing supplies safely across the Atlantic was sunk off Ireland on January 18, and on April 26 the ***Manchester Citizen*** (Capt. J. E. Everest) was lost on the same route.

On June 4 the ***Manchester Trader*** (ex-***Archenbloe***) engaged a submarine in a running fight in the Mediterranean before being sunk — a gallant action which was recognised by the awards to her master Capt. F. D. Struss and Chief Engineer W. R. Stobo, of the Distinguished Service Cross.

On the following day the ***Manchester Miller*** (Capt. W. A. Caldwell) was sunk 190 miles N.W. of the Fastnet, with the loss of eight lives.

During the First World War we adopted the ruse that when a ship was sunk another vessel was acquired and given the same name so that when, for instance, the enemy had received a report from his agents that the ***Manchester Inventor*** had been sunk off the Irish Coast in January, it became very difficult to reconcile it with the report that the same ship (actually ex-***Celtic King***) had arrived at Archangel on June 4, 1917, to be again sunk on July 30. The captain of the submarine, it transpired, normally traded in peacetime to the same pier in Montreal as the Liners.

The day before, the second ***Manchester Commerce*** (Capt. R. Smith) was sunk. Bought in 1916 as the ***King*** she only made one voyage to Archangel, and the Mediterranean.

Capt. F. D. Struss, DSC, OBE, an ML commodore, served the company for more than 40 years. He survived sinkings in both world wars

The ***Nation*** was acquired, transformed into the second ***Manchester Engineer*** (Capt. Owens) and made a voyage to Archangel. On her return she was sunk off the Tyne on August 16.

The ***Manchester Spinner*** (Capt. W. A. Caldwell) made two trips to the Mediterranean on Government Service in 1916, and in 1918 delivered supplies at Salonika. On her way home from the Far East she was sunk in the Mediterranean by an enemy submarine on January 22, 1918, and this fortunately, proved our last casualty.

The Liners could, however, give as well as take it, and in June, 1917, the ***Manchester Port,*** *en route* to Canada, beat off a submarine attack with gunfire. She had been taken over by the Sea Transport in 1915 for a voyage to Egypt, and later had delivered Admiralty coal to St. Vincent, Port Stanley and Callao.

The ***City*** continued through the war bringing fresh meat from the Argentine, and the ***Corporation, Shipper, Merchant*** and ***Exchange*** shuttled safely across the Western Ocean bringing supplies to France or Britain.

In 1917 the ***Manchester Mariner*** (Capt. J. Groth) sustained slight damage from a mine and put into Falmouth. However, she was able to continue her voyage to Leghorn with coal on a seaworthy certificate and the instructions "Captain, nurse her." Before returning home she towed the ***Labicum,*** a lame duck, 500 miles into Maderia.

The ***Manchester Brigade*** (Capt. J. R. Foale) and the ***Manchester Division*** which had been building at Messrs. Irvine's yard at West Hartlepool were added to the fleet. The new ***Division*** (Capt. E. W. C. Beggs), on her maiden voyage from West Hartlepool to join convoy at Plymouth rammed and sank a German submarine off Flamborough Head.

The conclusion of hostilities found the company, which had started the war with 15 ships, the owners of 12 vessels, despite its heavy losses.

Throughout the war the company continued its regular trade with Canada and in addition, in 1915, instituted a joint service to Baltimore known as the Furness-Johnston-Manchester Liners.

In 1919 Mr. R. B. Stoker died and Sir Frederick Lewis (who later became Lord Essendon) was appointed chairman; Mr. F. E. Vaughan, who had been secretary since the formation of the company, became managing director, and Mr. J. H. Poole was appointed secretary.

In 1920 the New Orleans service was resumed and the Baltimore service extended to serve Norfolk Va. In 1921 two vessels, the ***Start Point*** and the ***Grampian Range,*** were purchased and renamed ***Manchester Producer*** and ***Manchester Spinner*** respectively; the latter and the ***Civilian*** (which later after the Japanese earthquake in 1923 made several round trips under the command of Capt. Struss, with relief goods from the United States), subsequently became well-known in the Sydney C.B., coal trade.

The "Manchester Producer" (ex-"Start Point") was bought in 1916 and sold to the Board of Trade in 1939

In 1921 the company loaded the first ship on Furness, Withy's Pacific Coast service (which later became fortnightly) and played a great part in developing trade between this country and the western U.S.A. and Canada.

Requiring larger and more modern office accommodation the company bought a site next to the Royal Exchange in St. Anne's Square between 1920/21 and commenced to build a modern five-storey building which was named Manchester Liners House, into which they moved from their old premises in Deansgate in August 1922.

They also took delivery of their biggest ship, the ***Manchester Regiment,*** of 7,930 tons gross and 11,572 deadweight whose record from the Mersey to Quebec was seven days nine hours.

In 1925 the ***Manchester Commerce*** (Capt. J. R. Foale) and ***Manchester Citizen*** (Capt. J. Groth) were delivered.

The following year the ***Manchester Producer*** (Capt. G. M. Mitchell) while carrying a load of cattle, lost her rudder in a gale and was adrift in the Atlantic. After many unsuccessful efforts at salvage she was towed home by the ***Zwarte Zee*** from the Azores. Many cattle were killed as a result of heavy seas shipped and much publicity was given to this event.

The next year saw the disposal of the original ships, each of which had helped to make the port of Manchester known among the seamen of the world, the ***Manchester Mariner, Port*** and ***Exchange*** in 1925, the ***Importer*** in 1927, the ***Corporation*** in1929, the ***Shipper*** in 1930, and the ***Merchant*** in 1934. Faced with American subsidised ships on the route they had pioneered, it was impossible to maintain the same number of ships in this Philadelphia trade.

To replace the ***Manchester City,*** which had completed her useful life and was to be sold for breaking up, and to continue its interest in the River Plate trade, the company bought a half-share in the refrigerated motorship ***El Argentino.*** To maintain the American trade the ***Rexmore*** was acquired and became the ***Manchester Exporter.***

The original men were retiring, too; Capt. Foale, who won the gold-headed stick for first overseas arrival in Montreal in 1925 in the ***Manchester Regiment:*** Capt. Beggs, who later became president of the Mercantile Marine Service Association; Capt. J. E. Everest and Capt. W. J. Parry, and Mr. T. Mason Greenip, the superintendent, who was succeeded by Mr. Geo. Clay.

Then in 1929, in those days of safety first, came a story of great heroism at sea. The ***Manchester Regiment*** (Capt. Philip Linton) steamed 160 miles through a gale to reach the sinking Glasgow steamer ***Volumnia.*** A lifeboat was launched manned by Second Officer (now Captain) W. H. Downing, Third Officer (now Captain) E. W. Espley, Bo'sun J. Bromage, Able Seamen H. J. Stringer, Patrick Kearns, H. Chidlow, J. Manins and Mr. R. P. Ziegler, passenger. The crew of 45 doomed men were saved by "remarkable seamanship, skill and courage of the master, officers and crew of the ***Manchester Regiment***".

On return home the King awarded the Silver Medal for Gallantry in Saving Life at Sea to the officers and crew of the lifeboat, and the Lord Mayor of Manchester (Councillor R. Noton Barclay) presented a silver salver from the Board of Trade to Capt. Linton. In the hall of Manchester Liners was framed the resolution of the Manchester Ship Canal Company recording this "achievement which had stirred the imagination of the world and would ever be a source of inspiration to the whole nation, and of singular pride to the home port of Manchester."

KENNETH STOKER BECOMES MD

IN 1932, Mr. F. E. Vaughan died, and Mr. Kenneth Stoker, a director since 1919, became managing director. This was the time of depression, with several ships laid up, and in 1933 the ***Manchester Civilian*** was sold abroad; she was renamed ***Tasis*** and is believed to have been sunk off Naples in 1942. However, the services were still maintained and in 1935 the first of a new series of ships the ***Manchester Port,*** was launched from the yard of the Blythswood Shipbuilding Company, Scotstoun.

The year 1937 saw the new ***Manchester City,*** a tribute to her predecessor and, incidentally to the successful local football team, followed in 1938 by the ***Manchester Progress.*** These vessels, fitted with automatic stokers and equipped for carrying cattle, had special ventilation for fresh fruit, and particular attention was paid to the comfort of 12 passengers, while the crew's quarters were a great advance over earlier-type ships. The dock staff, who play a silent, unspectacular but most important part in the running of the line, also moved into a new and greatly improved dock office.

In 1938 the ***Manchester Regiment,*** in most unusual circumstances, was in collision with the ***Clan Mackenzie*** which sank in Liverpool Bay; this accident was long discussed in Liverpool shipping circles when the subject of compass adjusting was mentioned.

In 1939 the ***Manchester Producer*** was sold, becoming the ***Botwey,*** one of a number of ships purchased by the Board of Trade prior to the outbreak of war and given names with the appropriate prefix "Bot". Managed by P. Henderson and Co. Ltd., she was transferred to the Ministry of Shipping after the clouds of war broke, and was torpedoed and sunk by a submarine on July 26, 1941.

Because of their automatic stokers, which required special small coal, the Manchester Liners' fleet was largely retained on the Atlantic route. Because of their good speed and comfortable accommodation these well-found vessels were usually commodore ships and played a vital and unceasing part in the Battle of the Atlantic.

At the outbreak of the war the fleet comprised the following ships: ***Manchester Brigade*** (Capt. F. L. Osborne); ***Manchester Citizen*** (Capt. G. M. Mitchell); ***Manchester City*** (Capt. J. Barclay), ***Manchester Commerce*** (Capt. J. E. Riley); ***Manchester Division*** (Capt. E. E. Bonnaud); ***Manchester Exporter*** (Capt. G. S. Ronald); ***Manchester Port*** (Capt. F. D. Struss); ***Manchester Progress*** (Capt. P. Linton); ***Manchester Regiment*** Capt. W. E. Raper; ***Manchester Spinner*** (Capt. F. Clough).

Proceeding westbound without navigation lights in the winter of 1939 the ***Regiment*** (Capt. W. E. Raper) was sunk by the ***Oropesa*** — which vessel had been detached from an eastbound convoy for special duty — unfortunately with the loss of nine lives. A year later the ***Manchester Brigade*** (Capt. F. Clough) was torpedoed, taking all but four of the crew with her.

The ***Manchester Division*** (Capt. H. Hancock) *en route* for Table Bay received a signal on November 30, 1942, to proceed to the ***Dunedin Star*** which had been beached on an isloated and rugged coast with a very heavy swell and surf running. Forty-three members of the crew and 21 passengers, including seven women and three children, had been landed ashore in an exposed position. For three days, breaking wireless silence, the ***Division*** stood by and 40 crew and pasengers were taken aboard and landed in Capetown. In 1943 she made a voyage to New York, followed by several months' service in the Red Sea and Indian Ocean.

The ***Manchester City*** (Capt. J. Barclay) became a naval auxiliary minelaying "mother" ship until December, 1940, when she was transferred to the Admiralty; later she proceeded to the Indian Ocean, where she played her full part in the Far Eastern war.

The ***Manchester Progress*** (Capt. J. Barclay) returned independent of convoy in December, 1941, from Rangoon, being one of the last ships to leave this port, and fortunately escaped damage from patrolling Japanese 'planes. After a further voyage with supplies for the Eighth Army in the Middle East she returned to the Battle of the Atlantic and, in 1942, under Capt. Bonnaud, towed the motorship ***Forest***, then a "lame duck", several hundred miles towards the safety of Iceland without a naval escort and under very difficult conditions.

The ***Manchester Spinner*** was mainly on the Western Ocean, but in 1942 sailed on a nine months' voyage with supplies to India, under Capt. F. Downing. In 1944 she was sold for "special service" and under volunteer Capt. F. Lewis, this cradle of so many Manchester seamen led a line of blockships off the Normandy coast on June 7, 1944, to act as a breakwater to assist the landing of troops and stores on the beaches.

The ***Manchester Port*** made a trip under Capt. E. E. Bonnaud to the Middle East with supplies in 1941, and in November, 1942, equipped as a troopship and with landing craft aboard she landed the first troops and stores on Apple Beach near Algiers. She followed up with a second voyage.

In 1941 the ***Manchester Citizen*** (Capt. T. Makin) took supplies for the

This picture shows Mr. Kenneth Stoker (right) being presented with a gold wristle watch by his son, Mr. R. B. Stoker, marking over 40 years of service

Eighth Army and in 1942, under Capt. F. L. Osborne was one of the first ships to enter Bone on the North African coast and was under fire almost continuously for 16 days and nights. After two further trips under Capt. Swales she proceeded to the West Coast of Africa and was sunk by enemy action on July 9, 1943, with the regrettable loss of 15 lives.

The ***Manchester Trader*** was launched in 1941 and under Capt. E. W. Raper took her part, usually as commodore ship, in the Atlantic, except for a voyage to North Africa in December, 1942, and another one to Bone in September, 1943.

The new ***Manchester Merchant*** was delivered in May, 1940, and was on North Atlantic service until February, 1943, when, on her return from Algiers, she was torpedoed and 36 of her crew were lost. Capt. F. D. Struss, commodore of the Manchester Liners since the retirement of Capt. P. Linton, was rescued by a corvette after being in the water for some time. Capt. Struss was honoured with the O.B.E.

The ***Manchester Commerce*** also played her part in the North African invasion, making two trips under Capt. C. A. Walker. When commodore ship, she was attacked by enemy aircraft off Gibraltar, three of which were brought down. In 1943 she made a further trip to Alexandria. Next voyage was to Syracuse and she then proceeded to New York, from where Capt. W. H. Downing took her to India with mules; she spent most of the next year ferrying mules from South Africa to India.

The new oil-burning turbine vessel ***Manchester Shipper***, with accommodation for 75 passengers as a wartime measure, was delivered in October 1943. Except for one voyage to the Middle East, she continued under Capt. Struss on the North Atlantic.

The ***Manchester Exporter*** was first under Capt. G. Ronald, also on the North Atlantic run. Under Capt. W. H. Downing, she was hit by a tanker in Belfast Lough in December, 1942, and so much damage was done that only due to good seamanship was she saved. Afterwards, under Capt. F. Downing, she took supplies to Syracuse for the Sicilian invasion and later supplies for Naples, which had just been captured.

In addition to running their own ships the Liners managed and found key officers for the ***Belwoods Park*** (Capt. E. W. Espley), ***Riverdale Park*** (Capt. F. L. Osborne) and ***Westmount Park*** (Capt. M. E. Bewley), built as part of Canada's war effort. As regular ship agents at Manchester were unable to cope with the increased use made of the port, many outside vessels were handled by the company's hard-working and depleted staff.

In 1944 Lord Essendon died and was succeeded as chairman by Mr. (now Sir) Ernest Murrant, K.C.M.G., M.B.E., who had recently returned from the appointment of representative of the Ministyr of War Transport in the Middle East.

Peace came in 1945. Manchester Liners had started the war with 10 ships; five had been lost, but three new ships had been built, so that the company was able immediately to resume its weekly Canadian service.

In 1946, the ***Manchester Shipper*** made history by being one of the first merchant ships in peace-time to fit radar and to navigate the St. Lawrence River with its aid. So successful was this test that all the ships on this service were so fitted. In the same year also the company was honoured by carrying the Lord Mayor of Manchester and his official party to Canada on their goodwill mission.

The ***Manchester Exporter*** was sold in January, 1947, a month before delivery of the new ***Manchester Regiment***, an improved sister ship of the ***Shipper***. This vessel was presented by

Cammell Laird and Co. Ltd., Birkenhead, delivered the "Manchester Spinner", third of the name, in 1952

that famous unit of the regular forces — the Manchester Regiment — with a plaque of their badge, a *fleur-de-lys*, below which is the inscription: "This is the badge of the Manchester Regiment. It is placed here by the Regiment to commemorate the naming of the ship by Mrs. Dorling, wife of the Colonel of the Regiment, on October 16, 1946".

In 1947 the ships of the Furness Pacific coast service, for which Liners had acted as loading brokers since its inception, were berthed additionally on Harrison's West Indies service; this meant a big extension of shipments from Manchester and a corresponding increase in the loading work of Manchester Liners' staff. In addition, Liners attended to the tankers of the Esso Petroleum Co. Ltd. (formerly the Anglo-American Oil Co. Ltd.) in the port.

Earlier that year the Hon. Bona Dussalt retired: he became the company's St. Lawrence pilot in 1912 and, entering public life, rose to the position first of Minister of Agriculture; then Minister of Municipal Affairs in the Government of Quebec.

It was appropriate that on the golden jubilee of the company Capt. J. Barclay, of the ***Manchester Shipper***, should win the gold-headed cane for opening Spring navigation at Montreal; assisted by radar he beat his nearest competitor, an Italian ship, by 350 miles.

The year before the captain had missed the gold-headed cane by 15 minutes and was awarded a cane with a mourning bow. In 1933 he was awarded a cane of sugar candy.

In 1948, with only eight ships left, Manchester Liners embarked on a rebuilding programme to replace their war losses. After the delivery of the ***Manchester Merchant*** in 1950, an order had been placed with Cammell Lairds for the ***Manchester Spinner***, an even speedier, and as prices continued to rise, costlier vessel. But before the ***Manchester Spinner*** was delivered in 1952, the decision was taken to enter the Great Lakes trade.

This trade had been carried on by European operators since before the war, but British owners had not previously entered the trade, partly because British manning requirements were higher — and space on a small ship was at a premium — and partly because the westbound trade from the United Kingdom, as distinct from the

Continent, had made it difficult to obtain full westbound cargoes.

Due to the insistent demand from inland Canadian importers and exporters for ships to sail to their inland ports, and with the inevitability of the St. Lawrence Seaway, two specially designed small ships were ordered to start the first all-British service to Toronto. Thus, in the spring of 1952, the big ***Manchester Spinner*** slid down the ways, followed a few minutes later by the miniature ***Manchester Pioneer***; this dual launch was an historic event for Birkenhead. A few weeks later the ***Manchester Explorer*** joined her sister in the Mersey yard, and the new service began as had happened before with misgivings on Merseyside.

Symbolic perhaps of the new age, the ***Manchester Spinner*** did not waste time going up to the measured mile in Scotland but ran her trials with a Decca Navigator off the North Wales coast; while in the first cargo loaded on the ***Manchester Pioneer*** direct for Toronto was the first commercial "Electronic Brain" produced in Britain by Ferranti Ltd., for the University of Toronto . But before the new little ships reached Toronto the ***Manchester Merchant*** had opened the Port of Montreal.

A fast new Norwegian vessel had arrived at Quebec to proceed to Port Alfred in Saguenay River. As the river was closed by ice and the vessel had a few days to wait the owners decided to send the new ship to Montreal, open the port, collect the gold-headed cane, and considerable publicity.

She moved up the river but was compelled to return as the ice was still too thick. A day or two later the ***Manchester Merchant*** arrived in the evening and dropped anchor a little farther up river. Capt. Raper's information on the state of the ice was good, and very quietly during the night the ***Manchester Merchant*** slipped away. Six hours later the faster Norwegian vessel realised that the ***Manchester Merchant*** was no longer at anchor, and sailed in hot but useless pursuit.

The Norwegian vessel arrived in Montreal 20 minutes after the ***Manchester Merchant*** and proceeded back light to the Saguenay, without using the invitation cards which rumours said had been printed to invite guests to welcome her as the first arrival.

Capt. A. Starmer in the ***Manchester Pioneer*** had the warmest of welcomes for the first British service in the Lakes. He brought to Toronto a ship's bell,

Also built by Cammell Laird in 1952, the "Manchester Pioneer" was specially designed for the St. Lawrence Seaway trade

presented by the Manchester Chamber of Commerce, which still calls to order the members of the Toronto Board of Trade. Britain appeared much nearer to the inland British-settled province of Ontario. At one small place the town band turned out to welcome the new ship; as it was Saturday afternoon the members came directly from their allotments in shirtsleeves.

Because of the new saving in freight costs new orders were placed with Britain and new British factories came to Toronto or Hamilton, bringing in their plant direct from Manchester. The idea of a service from one inland port to another captured the imagination of the Canadians.

The first vessel discharged more overseas cargo into Toronto than the port had handled before from any single ship. For previous foreign ships it had been a port of call *en route* for Chicago with correspondingly small cargoes. With the limited facilities and labour there arose the problem of congestion but this was tackled energetically, and soon the Liners' service became an established favourite. The little ships with cream superstructure and maroon hulls attracted a continuous crowd at the foot of Bay Street.

It was a gay adventurous summer, with the Red Ensign pushing up creeks and muddy rivers where it had never been before. The vessels, trimmed to 14 ft. draft, would proceed through 21 locks inwards, with 6 in. to spare, and taking the current with them would coast down the deeper rapids and lock back through 18 locks. As the vessel approached the lock, the most athletic member of the crew swung ashore from the special lakes boom up forward and then in plimsolls ran ahead of the vessel to secure her in.

That summer the ***Manchester Explorer*** was ordered to load at Wallaceburg, a little town up the Sydenham River between Lakes Erie and Huron. There was a strike at the time which was suspended as the first British vessel arrived and resumed directly afterwards. Capt. Freeman, the Resident Superintendent of Furness, Withy and Co. Ltd., wrote the following description in the log of the ship's arrival: —

"After discharging her outward cargo the ***Manchester Explorer*** proceeded through the Welland Canal westwards towards Wallaceburg, which is near Detroit. I drove through to Wallaceburg ready to meet her on arrival. Now neither the vessel nor myself had been to this port so we were strangers to that part of the country.

"On my arrival that evening I began to explore the surrounding and was amazed to find a tiny wooden wharf alongside a narrow strip of water, which I learned later was the River Snye . . . I found the usual squatters, and diplomatically made enquiries

Sir Leslie Roberts, CBE, whose son Tony Roberts, became chairman and managing director of Manchester Liners. Sir Leslie served on the board from 1947 to 1975

about the waterfront. When informed that the local ships turned off the wharf I had grave doubts that this procedure would be carried out with the ***'Explorer***.

"At 7 p.m. the following day, August 11, the vessel moored, but it took an hour to turn her round and this was done in front of the Mayor and over 100 townspeople on the wharf and many more on the other side of the river and across the two bridges. The ***Manchester Explorer*** steamed through the narrow bridge, branches sweeping decks and bridge as she passed through with inches to spare.

"By the time the stern had cleared the road bridge the bow was close to the piles set in the grass lawn in the park, where the head rope had to be made fast to facilitate turning the vessel around.

"During this manoeuvre the stern came closer to the wharf and I could see that the ship had to move at least 10 ft. ahead. Suddenly I was aware that the bow was underneath the trees in the park on the other side of the river. Branches snapped sharply as the vessel tried to go ahead those few feet.

"Capt. J. L. McLaren shouted some instructions to the chief officer on the forecastlehead. The chief officer's head appeared among the branches which enveloped the after end of the forecastlehead. He said: 'We are all tangled up in the trees here'.

"I apologised to the Mayor, who was standing with me, for breaking his trees. He replied: 'Don't worry, they need pruning anyway'. Eventually the vessel was berthed and people went on board to welcome the ***Manchester Explorer*** to the city and port. She was the first British ship ever to berth there.

"After the welcome the townspeople invaded the vessel. At 11 p.m. we had managed to clear the decks of visitors. Loading began next day and finished the following day, August 13, at 12.30 p.m. At 1.15 p.m., the ***Manchester Explorer*** left Wallaceburg with the air full of 'Good-byes'."

Next winter, in order to satisfy shippers, the small Norwegian "Laker" ***Vigor*** was acquired, and renamed ***Manchester Prospector***. She was extensively refitted and joined her two consorts but not only on the Canadian Lakes. As these vessels could only load to 14 ft. in the Canadian Lakes, calls were developed for further loading down river below Montreal to Preston and Ardrossan from such ports as Chicoutimi, Rimouski, St. Anne des Monts, Grande Vallee or Campbellton.

In the spring of 1954, the Commodore of the Fleet, Capt. F. Struss, set off for Montreal in the ***Manchester Spinner***. The captain had spent over 40 years navigating this route without accident and could "smell the ice". Picking her way through the ice drifting out of the Gulf of St. Lawrence, the ship arrived at Quebec shortly behind an icebreaker which had cut a channel up to Montreal.

Capt. Struss took his vessel up this channel, the wash dislodging the ice still adhering to the shore. the broken ice drifted down astern, making an impassable barrier for a week. On March 30, Capt. Struss docked in Montreal, without the aid of tugs which were still frozen in. This was the earliest date since the days of Jacques Cartier that the port had been open.

The ***Manchester Spinner*** discharged, loaded, and passed the next ships coming up as she sailed down. Because of recent tragic cases of masters on their last voyages piling their ships ashore, the company decided not to tell a master when he was in fact on his last voyage.

Capt. Struss therefore, with his life's ambition fulfilled, and with a wonderful record, arrived home to retire. A year later the fleet mourned the death of its last commodore who gained his "ticket" in sail.

If the ***Manchester Prospector*** was not the first British ship to load out of Leamington, she was the first anyone could recall. Her arrival was a red-letter day at the small port.

CONVAIR RESCUE

ON August 5, 1954, a giant 10-engined RB36 Convair bomber was 450 miles West of Ireland on her way from California to Suffolk. She sent out an SOS to say her engines had caught fire, and as she came down in the Atlantic at 3.40 a.m. her crew of 23 were ordered to jump.

Immediately the American Air Force and the R.A.F. began to comb the area. At 11.36 a.m. some wreckage and survivors were sighted by an air-sea rescue plane which dropped a lifeboat. A flying boat was sent into the area but the sea was too rough for it to land. The weather grew worse and the ceiling lower so that even low flying aircraft were unable to see anything.

The ***Manchester Shipper*** with Capt. W. H. Downing, was en route to Manchester when the SOS was received. As she was within 100 miles of the scene she altered course and steamed at full speed for the position. At 12.15 p.m. a searching 'plane appeared and signalled the ***Manchester Shipper*** to follow her. At 1.28 p.m. the huge wings — 230 ft. long — of the wrecked aircraft came into sight, at first on radar. A lifeboat and dinghy were then sighted.

The ship's motor lifeboat, commanded by Chief Officer Fielding pulled away and rescued a survivor from the yellow lifeboat. After examining other wreckage and finding two bodies the lifeboat was recalled at 3.30 p.m. due to the weather becoming worse.

In the meantime, moving in the opposite direction was the ***Manchester Pioneer***, 150 miles away. Capt. A. Starmer turned her back and guided by aircraft came on the scene about 4 p.m. From 4.30 till 8.30 the ***Manchester Pioneer*** searched, finding a lifeboat with two survivors, and later a third in a dinghy.

The ***Manchester Pioneer*** was equipped with radio-telephone and so was able to communicate with the aircraft and the ***Manchester Shipper***, and three other vessels which had arrived. Accordingly, a manoeuvre reminiscent of convoy days was carried out. Capt. Starmer arranged this fleet to sweep the waters for 10 miles West at an interval of 10 cables, but darkness and rising seas prevented further results.

When the ***Manchester Pioneer*** arrived in Montreal she received a most enthusiastic welcome; the three American airmen were thankful for the Manchester seamanship and hospitality.

When the ***Manchester Shipper*** arrived at Eastham, she was met by senior officers of the American Air Force, who apart from interviewing St. Sgt. Speer, the survivor, analysed closely the whole rescue operations and all the difficulties encountered. There is no doubt that many valuable lessons were learned in sea-air co-operation, and the use of picking up survivors by nets was stimulated. The following letter was received from Major General Francis H. Griswold, H.Q. Third Air Force, APO 125, U.S. Air Force:

"This letter is to express my appreciation and gratitude for the aid from your concern in the recent RB-36 rescue mission. The ***Manchester Shipper*** aided the surface rescue operations by picking up one survivor and two bodies from the crashed RB-36 and delivering them to Liverpool, England. The ***Manchester Pioneer*** also aided the surface rescue operations by picking up three survivors and carrying them on to Montreal, Canada.

"These feats were done under adverse weather conditions with high seas and high winds. Your vessel also provided homing signals to guide other surface vessels to the area of the wreckage. After picking up our survivors, your vessels rendered all first aid possible and made the men as comfortable as possible. The U.S.A.F. shall long remember this aid in our time of need.

"Mr. Everall, of your London Office, was exceedingly helpful in dispatching and relaying messages, which contained vital information relative to the rescue operations from the vessels to my Rescue Control Centre.

"Please express my gratitude to the officers and men of the ***'Shipper*** and the ***'Pioneer*** and to Mr. Everall".

Brig. Gen. James C. Selser, Jnr., H.Q.7th Air Division N.Y. wrote in a similar strain.

Another service to Churchill, Manitoba, was begun in the meantime, during the short season. This was the second British service and the first from the West Coast. The first year sailings were made by the ***Cairnavon***, and the second year by the ***Manchester Progress***, which also loaded a general cargo from Churchill. The service was greatly appreciated by the grain importers.

For many years before the First World War Manchester Liners had pioneered the Gulf and South Atlantic trade, and it was decided to resume this old connection below Cape Hatteras. The service combined with the Virginian tobacco service, and was the only British one to the ports of Charleston, Savannah and Jacksonville. The service proved most popular with round-trip passengers seeking to escape the rigours of winter.

At the same time Liners were actively concerned with the establishment of the first British independent air cargo service across the Atlantic. Airwork Ltd., in which Furness, Withy and Company had a substantial stake,

Capt. Fred Downing, who succeeded his brother, Capt. W. H. Downing, as commodore. The brothers joined Manchester Liners as apprentices in 1913. For both to become commodore was a remarkable achievement

approached the line to act as their general agents in the Manchester area.

The company agreed if Airwork would put its aircraft into Ringway Airport, Manchester. Within a few weeks the Manchester tonnage was the biggest from all British and European ports; the future looked bright.

The first 'plane carried a tractor to New York, and later Donald Campbell's ***Bluebird*** was also carried to the U.S.A. But without assistance from the Government to carry mails or passengers the service was stopped, and foreign operators reaped where Manchester Liners had sown.

However, the extra staff was absorbed by the extension of the Lakes Service to Chicago, and the ***Manchester Explorer*** in October 1955 was the first British ship to report to the British Consulate in the hundred years since its establishment.

In the spring of 1955 Capt. F. L. Osborne, this time commanding the ***Manchester Spinner***, opened the Port of Montreal on April 2 — the first time any vessel had done this twice in two years.

In 1956 Montreal was opened on April 2 by the ***Manchester Regiment***, commanded by Capt. F. Downing, who had spent all his life on this trade. Following the big ship, the ***Manchester Explorer*** was the first British ship to load out to Chicago, and the publicity was nationwide and a fillip to trading morale.

A month later appeared the first two motorships of the line, the ***Manchester Vanguard*** and ***Manchester Venture***. In order to begin a service in the spring, these vessels were built by the A. G. Weser Company. Engines and accommodation were aft and with their big holds they quickly made a sound reputation.

With five small ships, the problem of employment in the winter months was a formidable one, and an arrangement was made with the Yeoward Line — also founded incidentally in 1898 — for the ***Manchester Vanguard*** and ***Manchester Venture*** to trade to the Canary Islands for tomatoes and bananas. The ships became very popular with shippers.

In 1957 the Commodore, Capt. E. W. Raper, guided the ***Manchester Mariner*** into Montreal, winning the Gold Cane for the second time, a feat which had never been achieved before by the same captain. The line had secured this honour six times since 1948, and for four successive years, a feat difficult to surpass.

In September, the ***Manchester Trader*** played a vital part in another tragedy. Although far from the Azores, her radio operator picked up and relayed to Valentia the last vital message from the unlucky German sail-training vessel ***Pamir***.

There was considerable radio traffic. Valentia passed the message on to

The first "Manchester Venture", built in Germany in 1956, was one of the first two motorships in the fleet

The second "Manchester Miller" delivered in 1959, bridged the gap between conventional and container operations

Portishead who ordered radio silence, and the search was on. The owners of the ***Pamir*** were in touch with Manchester, who spoke to the master. Dr. Wachs cabled "Thank you for your very valuable information, as well as for your sympathy which we highly appreciated".

In 1958, the Diamond Jubilee Year of Manchester Liners Ltd., the company had 14 ships at sea, compared with eight 10 years previously. Three more ships were ordered.

The company had pioneered an inland port, helped Manchester to become one of the greatest ports in England and to transform the "Cottonopolis" of 60 years ago into a "city and port of a thousand businesses".

A new race of inland seamen had been raised who, in peace and war, proved worthy of the highest traditions of any port in the Kingdom.

The name of Manchester Liners stood as high as it had ever done and its policy of catering adequately to the needs of the importing and exporting communities of this great industrial district were maintained.

Ahead lay the challenge of the St. Lawrence Seaway — not an easy trade as competition would be severe and problems would abound.

The third "Manchester City" dated from 1964. She served the company until 1971, when she was sold to Korean owners

ST. LAWRENCE SEAWAY OPENS

MANCHESTER LINERS had pioneered trade into the Great Lakes, operating the first British service in 1952, responding to the needs of Canadian exporters and importers. Fast, small vessels were utilised, of some 1,600 gross tons, able to navigate creeks, rivers and locks. A service to Churchill, Manitoba, handled grain and other cargoes and in 1956, a service to Chicago was added.

At the start of 1959 the company owned 14 vessels totalling 75,850 gross tons, plus three larger vessels on order in anticipation of the opening of

Designed for service to St. Lawrence Seaway ports or as fruit carriers in the Mediterranean trade, the "Manchester Faith" was one of two sisters.

the St. Lawrence Seaway. It was realised that the Seaway would attract other shipping along a route which the company had made very much its own, and the development of other trades.

The ***Manchester Miller*** was delivered in 1959 from Harland and Wolff, Belfast. She was the last of the generation of turbine ships built for Manchester Liners, each one an improvement on its predecessor. With nearly 600,000 cub. ft. of space, flush decks and a speed of 18 knots, the ***Manchester Miller*** was ideally equipped to continue with the traditional fast-package trade between Manchester and Montreal.

Also ordered, from the Sunderland yard of Austin and Pickersgill — who had a ready berth — were the ***Manchester Faith*** and ***Manchester Fame***. These versatile ships, able to go through the Seaway, were additionally designed as fruit carriers to serve the Canary Islands or Mediterranean countries. Lard had been successfully carried, so special epoxy-lined tanks were fitted to hold edible oils.

The ***Manchester Faith*** was soon to achieve fame. When the St Lawrence Seaway was officially opened in 1959 she was the first into the Seaway, beating a large assembly of vessels.

Prior to the official opening of the Seaway the master of the ***Manchester Faith*** had brought his ship alongside a small passenger vessel on board which were many of the VIPs. They included Mr Kenneth Stoker as chairman of Manchester Liners and the chairman of Canadian Pacific who was so impressed by the ship that he ordered some similar vessels.

It was not known at the time whether grain cargo would flow from inland ports such as Chicago or whether the railway export rates from the interior to the sea water ports of the Gulf of St. Lawrence would prevent this. Both the ***Manchester Faith*** and ***Manchester Fame*** were able to go up through the Seaway but without enough deadweight for the grain.

Another new service was established from Manchester, up to the head of the Great Lakes, to test whether the grain cargo market would be successful from there. The grain did start to flow.

This service was probably launched years ahead of its time. The first vessel had less than 50 tons of cargo for Port Arthur, but, over the years the service made Manchester Liners a household name in the prairie provinces. For a long time it was the only service from the UK and Europe to Duluth.

When the grain started moving, the Lakes vessels became bigger and bigger and, for a time, there was the spectacle of Liberty-type vessels in ballast, suffering from "windage" problems seeking a bonanza in the new trading area — for which they had neither the equipment nor the experience. A great deal of damage took place, and the vessels were also delayed by bunching and congestion.

Underwriters consequently put very heavy premiums on Great Lakes trade and this soon produced a very different picture.

As a result of trading by Manchester Liners to Duluth a tank farm for edible oils was built there. The ***Manchester Progress*** took the first cargo of edible oils out of Lake Superior in 1960.

During 1960 there was an unofficial seamen's strike, which lasted for six weeks, from July to September. The effects were particularly severe in Liverpool and on the North East Coast and among the stewards of passenger liners.

It is noteworthy that Manchester Liners were able to sail every single vessel throughout the six-week period. If short of crews, the vessels were sailed to other anchorages and crews recruited — or flown over as soon as they were available. In one case, a vessel sailed by signing on the pickets.

The "Manchester Prospector", formerly the Norwegian "Vigor", was bought in 1953 for the Great Lakes trade.

One reason for the fact that Manchester Liners sailed nine vessels during the strike is possibly the fact that the company paid great attention to the excellence of shipboard cuisine.

When the ***Manchester Prospector*** was bought, the company was worried about crews crossing the Atlantic in such a small vessel and decided to do everything possible to ensure that, on all vessels, the men were compensated gastronomically. In addition, steps had been taken in other ways to make the ships as self-contained as possible, for example by the installation of television sets. These moves did seem to pay off.

It was a great credit to the devotion of the officers, the marine department and the Shipping Federation that vessels were able to get away so successfully. The sixties did seem the decade for strikes. In 1961 there was a long dock strike in Toronto. Another problem in the same year came in the Manchester Ship Canal when the large sand-hopper ***Mary P. Cooper*** was in collision near Warrington, sinking to the bottom. It was extremely difficult to get her up again.

It was suggested to the canal company that she should be blown up but there were fears for the windows of neighbouring houses. Eventually, with the aid of salvage "camels", she was hauled away after a month's work. The ***Manchester Progress*** which had been waiting laden with cargo at Irlam and all the other trapped vessels were at last able to proceed.

The ***Manchester Vanguard*** and ***Manchester Venture*** were chartered out in various directions and in the fruit trade and eventually sold to the General Steam Navigation Company in 1961. At the same time the ***Manchester Prospector***, which had been on the Maritimes run, for lumber, was also sold.

The larger vessels and regular services into the Lakes were starting to build up traffic. An order was placed for the ***Manchester Commerce*** for 1964, the largest and fastest vessel ever owned in the Port of Manchester at the time, especially designed for the edible oil trade.

The ***Manchester Commerce*** was fitted forward with a TV monitoring camera to assist docking. She created a great impression for her facilities, not least those for handling cargo. Her master was Capt Fred Downing, who had been commodore for two years, following the retirement in 1959 of his commodore brother, Capt W. H. Downing. Both joined the company as apprentices in 1913 and achieved this remarkable record.

It had been hoped that the ***Manchester Fame*** and ***Manchester Faith*** would be able to spend their winter months in the Canary Islands trade carrying tomatoes and bananas. Agreement was made with Yeoward Bros., Liverpool, for this, but problems were encountered with the Spanish authorities, including their putting up the speed requirement for carrying tomatoes to 16 knots. As a result the company had to withdraw from its association in this trade with Yeowards, who then became agents for the Spanish Aznar Line.

Another service commenced at the time was that of taking whisky from Glasgow to Miami and Southern States of the USA, a great boost to the whisky trade. This was profitable for a number of years but eventually attracted competition from Continental lines **en route** to the Gulf of Mexico, who started calling in also. There was enough business to support one line but when the sailings reached several a month the trade ceased to warrant it and the service was ended in 1967.

The company had also turned its attention to other services. The ***Manchester Pioneer*** was lengthened by another 40 ft. to help in carrying the amount of cargo being offered to Manchester Liners. The quantity continued to increase so the vessel was sold two years later, her place being taken by much larger chartered vessels.

The question of the trading of the company's smaller vessels had become a problem. The ***Manchester Explorer*** was fitted with a heavy derrick and

Largest and fastest vessel owned in Manchester at the time was the "Manchester Commerce" of 1964.

John Clarkson

The "Manchester Engineer" seen leaving Eastham Locks outward bound. She was the former Cairn Liner "Cairngowan."

found a useful job on charter to the Chimo Shipping Company, trading in the summer months from Montreal. Only British ships were allowed to trade coastwise.

Her voyages after the opening of the Seaway were probably among the most adventurous of any fleet. The list of her ports of call (if port they could be called) sounded like the exploration of the North West Passage — Port Chimo in Ungava, Frobisher Bay in Baffin Land, Coral Bay in Cape Dorset in the North of Hudson's Bay, and back to Goose Bay.

At all these remote ports in the North the cargoes were landed on to barges and taken ashore. The crews and the Eskimos worked together to discharge and load the cargoes.

Capt Fred Downing was succeeded as commodore by Capt E. W. Espley, who made his flagship the ***Manchester Miller*** on the Montreal rather than the Great Lakes run.

In these years of expansion Manchester Liners not only assisted the development of commerce in the Great Lakes but also in the lower St Lawrence. Machinery was carried for a new Canadian and British aluminium company in Baie Comeau; the first consignment of aluminium was brought back to the UK and regular calls continued. Newsprint was also carried.

Calls were made at lumber ports down river from Quebec — St Anne des Montes, Rimouski, Black Cape, Chatham, Newcastle and Campbellton, using chartered vessels after the smaller vessels had been sold.

The Furness Warren Line was introduced into the trade to and from St John NB where Manchester Liners held berth rights.

The ***Manchester Faith*** and ***Manchester Fame*** became part of a deal with the Cairn Line. The latter ship had just spent the winter on a very attractive cruise as far as the crew were concerned with KNSM out in Jamaica.

For the next two years the ***Manchester Faith*** became the ***Cairnesk*** and the ***Manchester Fame*** the ***Cairnglen***, trading as Cairn Line vessels out of the Tyne and Leith to Montreal. In return, Manchester Liners received the bigger Cairn Line vessels ***Cairngowan***, which became the ***Manchester Engineer*** and the ***Cairnforth***, which became the ***Manchester Freighter.*** These vessels continued to trade with Manchester Liners right up to 1969.

In the meantime, modernisation of the fleet was taking place. Early in 1964, in April, Capt W. G. Oliver took the ***Manchester Renown*** up the Lakes, followed in August by Capt J. T. Jones in the ***Manchester City***. This meant that Manchester Liners was able to give a very fast service through to Chicago.

By 1964 Canadian Government ice-breakers were operating in the winter, breaking up the ice to prevent flooding. Manchester Liners seized the opportunity to establish a year-round service, ordering the first of the company's ice-strengthened vessels, the ***Manchester Port*** and ***Manchester Progress***.

The background to this move was the fact that while, for many years, Manchester Liners had almost traditionally sailed the first vessels into Montreal after the winter season, the Danish Lauritzen Line, assisted by the work of the Government ice-breakers, had established a winter service through to Montreal.

But Manchester Liners refused to be left behind. The ***Manchester Port*** and ***Manchester Progress*** were not only designed to go in the winter to Montreal but also to carry lard from Chicago in vertical tanks in large hatches. Equipped with 30-ton cranes they were fast, with twin Pielstick engines, highly automated down below and fitted with remote control from the bridge.

By 1966 Manchester Liners had a fleet of 20 ships owned or chartered which operated on the North Atlantic or the Great Lakes. It was possible to run a year-round service to Montreal.

It was in that same year that another strike took place, called by the National Union of Seamen, lasting for 47 days from May 16 to July 1 and causing the Prime Minister to declare a State of Emergency. As the ships returned to the UK the crews left them and went on strike.

The ***Manchester Merchant*** was fortunate in that she left 24 hours before the strike for Canada. Unfortunately, there was also a strike of stevedores in Montreal, plus a strike of Seaway lock-gate men, so she spent two months in Montreal. The ***Manchester Freighter*** also spent 38 days in Toronto.

There seemed no point in settling the proposed terms in Canada as on the return of the vessels to the UK the men would have gone out on strike anyway. Finally, the Canadian Government insisted on a settlement.

The official strike of seamen had other repercussions. For decades the Anchor Line had shared the whisky business to New York from Glasgow with United States Lines. Suddenly, their ships were out of action. Into the gap came Sea-Land, offering containers — and the security which containers could provide. The days of the Anchor Line on the North Atlantic were numbered.

Glasgow was traditionally the home of the Donaldson Line, a family firm which also operated out of Bristol. Their main cargo was whisky for the Canadian Liquor Commission. A deal was made for the Cairn Line to withdraw Leith sailings and to have a share of the Glasgow trade with the Donaldson Line, who had teamed up with the Head Line, the latter acting as Glasgow agents. Manchester Liners, as successors to the Cairn Line, came into the Clyde.

In the meantime, the ***Manchester Progress*** — before being sold to the Yugoslavs for breaking up — carried in her last year the rather quaint cargo of six 1885-vintage narrow-guage locomotives from Penrhyn Quarries, destined for a miniature railway museum in Virginia. She was replaced by the ***Manchester Port.***

As a temporary expedient, the fleet was increased by the ***Manchester Exporter,*** which had been the ***Cairndhu***. She traded successfully, particularly up to the head of the Lakes, until 1969.

While there was no longer the same distinction in getting the first vessel into Montreal after the winter, there were prizes for the first ships of the New Year, with all the Canadian and American Lake ports making presentations.

In 1966 the ***Manchester Commerce*** was the first into Toronto, beating a Russian vessel. In the same year the ***Manchester Shipper*** received a "first" plaque in Chicago. In the following year the ***Manchester Commerce*** was second into Toronto, while the ***Manchester Exporter*** gained three "firsts", in Hamilton, Port Arthur and Toledo.

In 1968 Capt Lobban, master of the ***Manchester Engineer*** (ex-***Cairngowan),*** on charter to Manchester Liners, not only received a "first" barometer at Port Arthur but also was greeted in Duluth by Miss Minnesota.

In 1968 the Prince Line, which had served Manchester from 1894, decided to withdraw their Manchester service, which had been losing money, and were also thinking of closing the Mediterranean operations from London. It was felt that this would not help the overall position of the company and so Manchester Liners brought the Prince Line loading brokers, Gough and Crosthwaite, were given West Coast rights to the Mediterranean and started the Manchester Prince Line with long-term chartered ships which were renamed ***Trojan Prince, Spartan Prince*** and ***Tartar Prince*** — names, oddly enough, of the vessels running under the Prince Line service from the

The "Manchester Shipper" transiting the Manchester Ship Canal. Built in 1943, she served the company until 1969, when she was broken up at Trieste.

John G. Callis

Sold to Liberian-flag operator in 1968, the "Manchester Merchant" was renamed 'Clio".

Mediterranean to the USA at the turn of the century.

The Prince Line vessels had been run rather like yachts with a lot of passenger space, the best cargo space being taken up by accommodation. By chartering smaller ships and "creaming" the trade it was possible to make money. The success of these policies led to the Prince Line services from London being offered to Manchester Liners, but ML were so involved in the build-up towards containerisation on the North Atlantic that this offer was declined. However by the adoption of similar policies, the Prince Line services from London were reprieved, to the upset of competitors.

There was a problem of finding homeward cargoes, so the Golden Cross Line and the Constantine Line were also acquired by Manchester Liners in order to extend trading operations and opportunities in the Mediterranean. These acquisitions gave invaluable experience of the Mediterranean as a trading area. After a few months the homeward berth from Italy was suspended although space continued to be offered for a time from Sicily.

At a later date, at the start of the 1980s, the Italian trade was revived in combination with other ports, so perhaps the £10,000 paid for the rights was then justified.

During the 1960s the company continued to develop new trades by setting up joint services with other companies. One, with the Bristol City Line, was projected as a route from Manchester and the Bristol Channel to the USA. However delays and shortages of labour in UK ports hit the service, which lasted for only a season.

More success attended a joint venture started in 1967 with Irish Shipping Ltd for cargo to the USA and Canada. This go-ahead company was an old friend. In the early 'fifties Manchester Liners had co-operated with them in the carriage of frozen Irish meat to the USA until such time as they had their own reefer tonnage, and had also regularly time-chartered their vessels.

They were finding that the amount of general cargo from Dublin was insufficient to justify a good service but added to a UK port it made sense. Accordingly, as United States Lines had recently withdrawn from the Manchester - New York service, the breach was filled by using their vessels ***Irish Spruce*** and ***Irish Poplar,*** both with reefer cargo space, while the

Canadian berth was covered by the frequent Manchester ships on the way home.

Running the service was not too easy as, following the Devlin proposals, London and Liverpool went on protracted strikes and Manchester, although the port kept going, had one-day-a-week guerilla strikes, with a shortage of labour adding to delays. Later on, Irish Shipping took over the management of the services.

The year 1968 saw the growth of the company into a group. As Manchester Liners grew in size and interests so the need for service units became apparent for certain types of operations.

The ship repair firm of Morrell Mills and Co Ltd — the second oldest firm in Trafford Park, Manchester, having been founded in 1899 — was taken over, one of their subsidiaries being the old-established ships' caterers and provision merchants James Walker and Son (Shipping) Ltd., founded in 1865. A further acquisition at the time was that of Condron (Manchester) Ltd, boiler scalers and cleaners since 1910.

* * *

Manchester Liners lead into the container age

BY the middle of the 1960s Manchester Liners foresaw that the pattern of trade on the North Atlantic was likely to be dictated by the use of fully-cellular container vessels. Productivity among longshoremen was getting less, costs were continually rising and the shadow of the American container lines was looming across the North Atlantic.

Decisions worked out, in complete secrecy, were to result in Manchester Liners leading Britain into the container era, operating in 1968 the first British fully-cellular deep sea container vessel across the North Atlantic.

In fact, the seeds had been sown as far back as the late 1950s, when Manchester Liners began experimenting with better ways of carrying cargo. At that time, collapsible wooden containers were devised enabling cars to be carried three or four high in the lower holds: a contract having been secured with North American Van Line. Antique furniture was also carried in this way. Eight-foot square containers were then used, carrying car parts, especially for Ford.

In the early 1960s, continuing to look hard at methods of rationalising the company's own work and cargo handling, Manchester Liners, in conjunction with the Manchester Ship Canal Company, were the first to produce a pallet pool for exporters and also to send goods across the Atlantic secured on pallets.

It was in 1960 that Manchester became the first port to marshal export lorries into queues at the Manchester Liners berth to avoid the congestion and delays which lorries were experiencing at other ports.

After the 8ft. square containers, the company began building 10ft. containers. However it was clear that the requirement was for containers measuring in the region of 20ft., but the derricks of the time were not strong enough for containers of that size.

A pilot scheme for container handling was introduced. The ***Manchester Shipper,*** on the Chicago run, was fitted with a 30-ton derrick. The service ran for a trial period while the company gained experience in this new form of cargo handling. The first export Customs-approved depot in the UK was established at Water Street, Manchester, again with the co-operation of the Manchester Ship Canal Company.

Two main factors lay behind the decision to start a service to Chicago with containers. There was the increasing success of American shipping lines with this type of service from US ports to Hawaii or Puerto Rico — both

Built in 1967, the "Manchester Progress" was converted to a cellular container ship in 1971 and renamed "Manchester Concept."

in the American Customs Union and, therefore, free to develop without Customs problems — coupled with a proposal to extend these services across the Atlantic.

A number of international authorities were keen for such services across the Atlantic and the North Sea to expand trade through Europe. To make the rules easier for this type of movement, ISO standards were being worked out for an intermodal concept.

Productivity in the Canadian trade was continuing to fall, reaching 45 per-cent of the figures regarded as normal a few years previously; costs were rising and delays becoming more frequent.

As an example, the ***Southern Prince*** left Manchester on December 6, 1966, also later than scheduled, and returned in 84 days — but even this was only accomplished by sailing sideways in the ice through Quebec Bridge. The new ***Manchester Progress,*** with a combination of go-slow and ice, made a 90-day passage. It was clearly impossible to stay in business under these conditions.

The trends had been studied closely by ML's management for several years. At that time — the middle 1960s — no British shipping company had introduced the relatively new idea of containerisation.

The problem of the Canadian trade was that although much of the westbound cargo was suitable for containerisation, this did not seem to apply to eastbound cargoes, which were of a deadweight nature such as metals or raw materials with big internal transport problems.

In 1965 the writer flew to British Columbia as a British Chamber of Commerce delegate, meeting Canadian opposite numbers. He seized the opportunity to discuss the White Pass Yukon railway operations out of Vancouver, learning that the same problems had been faced with similar commodities — large amounts of heavy metals, not suitable for standard 20 x 8 x 8ft. boxes — and the difficulties had been overcome.

The answer was to go into half-height boxes so that twice the amount of cargo could go into the same standard space. Further discussions were held in Chicago and Montreal, after which Manchester Liners decided to set up a special containerisation study group.

Managing director Mr Tony Roberts, company secretary Mr Mark Pattison, and Mr J. A. Clay, chief marine and engineer superintendent, carried out intensive research into the problems of traffic, finance and technical feasibility. The group was briefed to produce a report on what it **was** possible to get into containers — not what it was impossible to get into any kind of container. The approach was that containers had to be adapted for cargo needs.

That left two top executives, Mr Christopher A. Skelton and Mr John R. Killick to keep the firm running on a day-to-day basis.

In the following year, while in Halifax, Nova Scotia, to address a weekend seminar for the Halifax Port Authority, the writer received attractive offers of credit from some foreign shipbuilders. It appeared that the ML project, conceived and still being carried forward in secrecy, was a starter.

British shipbuilders became fearful of foreigners gaining great commercial advantage from building container vessels. A director of Swan Hunter saw the Minister of Technology and, after investigation, the Shipbuilding Industry Assistance Act was passed. This not only prevented the South Bank yard, on the Tees, from going to the wall but provided an immense tonic for all major British yards.

Orders were placed at Smith's Dock Co. Ltd., Middlesbrough, for three fully-cellular container vessels, capable of carrying 500 20ft. equivalent containers, to be delivered in 1968-69. These were the first container ships to be ordered in British yards. Subsequently, the order was increased by a further cellular ship, while 10,000 containers were ordered from UK suppliers.

Total capital investment was about £16mn. It was realised that the greatest efficiency would be obtained through the control of two main and exclusive container terminals on either side of the North Atlantic, one sited in the Port of Manchester and the other at the Port of Montreal.

In conjunction with Furness, Withy and Co. Ltd a lease was taken out in Montreal for space necessary for the erection of container cranes, buildings and equipment. Furness in Montreal had been operating, from as long ago as 1898, as agents for Manchester Liners.

An agreement for a similar container terminal operation was effected in Manchester. The terminals and other facilities were designed to Manchester Liners own specifications. The necessary special equipment — gantry cranes, spreaders and van carriers had to obtained and container handling systems had to be worked out. The venture involved Manchester Liners in much pioneering work.

In an interview with Kenneth Brown, then editor, subsequently managing editor of the long-established daily shipping newspaper "Journal of Commerce and Shipping Telegraph" the writer pointed out that when first in the field with a new development there were no textbooks and no experienced staff to recruit.

"We had to start from scratch, train the staff and write our own textbooks", he said.

The secrecy of the containerisation project was preserved right up to the holding of a press conference in Manchester's Midland Hotel a year before the commencement of the service.

Even up to the start of the conference, steps had been taken to mislead. The main exhibit appeared to be an aeroplane, carefully concealed except for its nose. Betting ran high among the assembled journalists about a link-up between Manchester Liners and the then British European Airways. But the aeroplane was whisked away, a model container vessel was unveiled and the ordering of the container vessels was announced.

"What was that aeroplane doing there?", asked a perplexed correspondent, who looked as though his bet might have been on the losing side. It was explained that it had got there by mistake.

To save cabling expenses — and preserve secrecy — strange names had been invented to describe the different types of containers. They were called lions, tigers, hippos, mules and jumbos. The jumbos were 20ft. long standard containers, the mules half-heights for metals.

The growth of container units from a dozen or so in the beginning up to 2,000 a year did produce problems of control. A strike in the USA caused several hundred to be "lost" for a few weeks. Hiring replacements was a costly business.

In Manchester all-day sessions were held with the Manchester Ship Canal Company to make arrangements for a gantry crane, the terminal area, a weighbridge, an empty container park and a packing zone, all within the docks.

This concept was different from that which was fashionable. Manchester Liners endeavoured to find as many jobs as possible to avoid dockers being displaced with a view to getting cooperation on the project. A container repairing base was established by subsidiary Morrell Mills, sited behind the packing sheds, while the 4,500 containers for the three container vessels had to be planned bearing in mind the varieties of cargo and problems of extreme heat and cold.

The terminal in Montreal, on a site acquired from the National Harbours Board after sessions with the chairman in Ottawa, needed also to be ready in time, so a large gantry crane was ordered from Clyde, Booth and Crane, shipped out and erected. Arrangements were made for a giant snow shed to be built to protect containers during the Canadian winter, and a railway line put in at the back of the shed.

All this entailed directors and senior executives in almost "boxing and coxing" across the Atlantic.

At the same time, there was another pressing problem requiring attention. It had become obvious that the quiet, dignified building which formed the headquarters of Manchester Liners in St Ann's Square, Manchester, was

J. K. Byass

First of the new container ships, the "Manchester Challenge", built in 1968.

The original headquarters of Manchester Liners in St. Ann's Square, Manchester.

already practically bursting at the seams with the number of employees. It would certainly not be able to cope with the additional staff and facilities which were needed.

While luckless executives were trying to run conventional services, with all their delays, and to plan the new container services, a new Manchester Liners building had to be planned.

A four-acre site, former railway sidings between Nos. 8 and 9 Docks, was rented from the Manchester Ship Canal Company. A 10-storey building was designed, with the first four floors for tenants, a restaurant on the top floor, complete with a branch of Barclay's Bank, a hairdressing salon and a shop.

A sister building of six storeys in the same complex was planned for H.M. Customs, plus a Queen's Warehouse, the Customs also moving from the centre of Manchester. To complete the area, a car park was included, set in landscaped grounds, and a separate access road built.

Prior to the delivery of the container vessels the conventional vessels were gradually sold, the ***Manchester Regiment*** going in 1967 to become the ***Azure Coast II.*** She was followed by the ***Manchester Merchant,*** which became the ***Clio.*** In September 1968, the ***Manchester Spinner*** became the ***Estia*** and in 1969 the ***Manchester Mariner*** became the ***Ira,*** unfortunately sinking, a little later on, off the Amazon. Soon afterwards the ***Manchester Exporter*** went to new owners.

Capt Espley, who had played a wonderful part with the company as master and commodore, retired to be succeeded by Capt Starmer. This was also the period, of course, when the Manchester Prince Line, with its Mediterranean interests, was being developed.

On the North Atlantic, all the planning leading up to the introduction of containerisation from Britain by Manchester Liners was coming towards fruition.

The vessels under construction were being built to Lloyd's Class I ice-stiffening, together with additional stiffening to owner's requirements. An ice knife was specially designed and fitted aft over the rudder to protect the area in the event of the ship having to back into ice. A stabilising system was devised to prevent listing as vertical cells were discharged.

The design had to take into consideration the navigation of the Manchester Ship Canal to Manchester, carrying the maximum cubic and deadweight, while also ensuring that the canal passage would not be abnormally long. The engine room was designed for unmanned operation, the ship being controlled from the bridge, and reduced maintenance time in port was also taken into account, special arrangements making this possible.

Each of the 19½-knot vessels were to be of 12,000 tonnes deadweight, with 14 hatches and five separate cellular holds, with the capacity to carry 500 20 x 8 x 8ft. containers — 640,000 cub. ft. below deck, with the facility to include 40ft. containers.

It had been decided to carry all containers below deck — for three reasons: the North Atlantic weather could be very heavy, it was anticipated that container cargo be the "cream" — and St Lawrence winter ice produced its own problems.

The design of the container vessels was based, in great measure on the design of the ***Manchester Port*** and ***Manchester Progress***, plus all that had been learned from these vessels about Pielstick 16,000 hp engines and automation, the operation of unmanned night engine rooms.

The appropriately-named *Manchester Challenge,* the first vessel to be completed by Smith's Dock Co. Ltd., inaugurated the first British deep-sea fully cellular container vessel service, in November 1968 from the container terminal at the Port of Manchester to the container terminal at Montreal.

The *Manchester Challenge*, with Capt P. Fielding in command, arrived at Montreal in the worst snowstorm for many years. Cars could not be driven home and Canadian Director Peter Evans had to stay on board for the night. However, all the systems worked and the giant snow shed proved its worth. Because all the containers had been under-deck, insurance claims were negligible. The months of planning told.

Instead of sending cellular vessels up to Toronto, a deal had been made with Canadian National Railways, to hire a weekly train to take container cargo on flat cars to and from a new automated Concorde Terminal, near Toronto. Hamilton also became a major depot for the cargo. Onward movement was by truck or by other container trains from Chicago, Detroit, Winnipeg and other inland destinations.

The Montreal container terminal was opened by Mr Kierans, Canadian Government Postmaster General; assisted by Sir Colin Crowe, British High Commissioner; and Mr Howard Mann, chairman of the National Harbours Board.

Mr Peter Evans and Mr Rob Stoker attended the ceremony — and Mr Stoker recited his parody of Longfellow's "Hiawatha" which he had written especially for the occasion:

Mighty shipper, full of orders —
How to pack them is the problem
Pack them into cardboard boxes
Thieving hands will find their way in
Bricks will take the place of bottles
And the orders will go elsewhere;
Pack them into great wood boxes
From the forests full of fireflies
Mighty boxes — mighty costly
Better try the wooden pallets
Heap the cartons into pallets —
This improves but is not perfect;
Better try a new container —
Manchester Liners have 5,000 —
Pack them safely against the ocean,
Lock and seal the new container
Then those outside cannot get inside
And what is inside cannot get outside.
Insurance rates should be much lower
And the goods look freshly perfect.
When prairie shipper next goes hunting
His quiver comes back full of orders,
Mother of his father cries
"Now you have outsold Hiawatha!"

There was enormous publicity for the arrival of Canada into the container age — and Mr Stoker's parody was extensively quoted.

The next voyage of the ***Manchester Challenge*** was even more impressive. Although heavy ice and poor productivity had kept 37 vessels in Montreal for a month, she lost only two days. She berthed, discharged, loaded and left. The conventional ships were still in Montreal.

These voyages set the pattern for what was soon to become, by the summer of 1969, regular high-speed year-round container vessels services by Manchester Liners across the North Atlantic between Manchester and Montreal.

The subsequent sister vessels were named ***Manchester Courage, Manchester Crusade*** and ***Manchester Concorde.***

The ice-strengthening and extra power of the container vessels proved so effective that they regularly cleared passageways through the winter ice which were used by other vessels and even, on at least one occasion, went to the rescue of ice-breakers.

After a successful maiden voyage the ***Manchester Courage***, under Capt D. G. Thomas, had an unfortunate accident on March 16, 1969, developing a wild propeller and crashing through lock gates at Irlam. Immediate steps were taken to minimise the damage.

Within a week of the accident her container cargo was transferred to the ***Manchester Challenge*** at Liverpool. Meanwhile, the ***Hother Isle,*** a converted cellular ship, was chartered.

During the canal's closure the company's vessels used other ports, including Barrow, Glasgow and Hull, while go-slows and guerilla strikes delayed the ***Manchester Shipper*** for 34 days at Liverpool.

When a tug strike in the Autumn of 1969 paralysed the Port of Manchester for two weeks, the versatility of the container system was shown, two vessels discharging and loading at Greenock with no delay.

Trade was continuing to grow so it was decided that a fourth vessel, to be bare-boat chartered from the Nile Steamship Company should be ordered to enable a "conveyor belt" 4½-day sailing frequency to be maintained by the end of 1970. Another decision was to convert the ***Manchester Miller,*** which was still a fairly young vessel, to carry containers.

All this meant that the veteran ***Manchester Shipper*** went off for scrap, the ***Manchester Pioneer*** was sold to a Panamanian company, becoming the ***Halieto Oceano;*** and the ***Western Prince,*** which had been on charter since 1961, went back to her owners. Cargo was being attracted to and from the Continent, even as far away as North Italy.

The company was continually on the look-out for more sources of cargo — and means of transporting it efficiently — to fill the impending 4½-day North Atlantic container vessel frequencies.

In 1969 this resulted in the introduction of another first, the "Flying Fish" air, land and sea services, carrying cargo to distant destinations faster than all-sea, cheaper than all-air.

The concept was based on a simple premise, that if you place a piece of string across a globe from one point to another — the Great Circle line — it would in many cases go through

Port of Manchester container terminal at No. 9 Dock, with the "Manchester Courage" alongside.

Manchester. This applies, for example, to the Great Circle line from Mexico to Beirut, or Los Angeles to Kuwait.

Cargo could be flown from these faraway countries to airports at Montreal or Manchester taken on by fast container vessels across the North Atlantic and flown on to the ultimate destination.

The company was air orientated, having been agents for the Air Work Atlantic service in the 1950s for a year or so.

Mr Leslie Castlemaine, a businessman and pilot of considerable distinction — he had flown many types of aircraft and at one time was a member of the famous pioneer aviator Sir Alan Cobham's team — was recruited to manage the company's Flying Fish Division.

Within a few weeks European traffic was being flown into Manchester, carried by sea to Montreal and then flown on to Los Angeles and even New Zealand and Central America. Sales offices were established on the American West coast and later in Mexico and in the Mediterreanean.

Manchester Liners thus became the first truly intermodal transport company. In 1971 the company signed interchange agreements with Air Canada and subsequently with CP Air.

The key to all these developments: the year-round twice-weekly regular efficient and cost saving fully-cellular containership services between Manchester and Montreal, crossing the North Atlantic in 6½ days — and from Montreal to United States and Canadian Great Lakes ports, served by feeder container vessels based at the Canadian "gateway" port.

Exporters were finding that the new container service reduced transport time by up to 75 per cent, cut pilferage and damage and — mainly because of under-deck stowage — reduced insurance claims by 99.5 per cent over conventionally-stowed goods. There were stabilising effects on transportation costs which would otherwise have gone up to such an extent as to have a disastrous effect on export markets.

(to be continued)

The "Manchester Concorde", one of the original four cellular container vessels ordered by the company and delivered in 1969.

MANCHESTER LINERS HOUSE OPENED

ON December 12, 1969 His Excellency Mr. Charles S. A. Ritchie C.C., High Commissioner for Canada, officially opened the new Manchester Liners House, an elegant 10-storey building situated only a quarter of a mile from the container terminal.

At the suggestion of the writer, the building was designed in a curve to symbolise the bridge of a ship, modelled on the bridge of the ***Manchester Miller***. Appropriately, Mr Ritchie swung a bottle of champagne against a front pillar before unveiling a plaque and declaring the building open.

Included in the complex, a new Customs Hall containing a long room for goods clearance and a Queen's Warehouse for impounded goods, twin parks for over 250 cars — and a self-service petrol station, named Maple Leaf garage.

Canadian links are obvious. At the main entrance stands a 32ft. high Canadian Indian totem pole, specially carved for Manchester Liners at the request of Mr. Rob Stoker by Douglas Cranmer, of the Kwakiutl tribe of Indians, British Columbia.

The pole has four symbolic representations — the eagle, ruler of the skies; the killer whale, master of the seas; the raven, a messenger symbolic of trade; and a chief holding copper, indicating the wealth and power appropriate to a chief.

In the foyer, is a carving depicting a polar bear fighting a sea monster. The carving, a gift from Furness Withy and Company, the then general agents in Canada for Manchester Liners, was the work of an Eskimo named Mikigeeak, of Cape Dorset, Baffin Island.

Also in the foyer, is a 14 x 7ft. mosaic depicting marine life, the materials used being pebbles, sea glass, broken pottery from garden and seashore, abalone shells from the Californian coast and stones from a Scottish river bed.

The mosaic was designed and created by Eleanor Mather — Lady Mather, wife of Manchester industrialist Sir William Mather. In the restaurant is a mural depicting Canadian life, scenery and people, designed and painted by David Stoker, son of Mr Stoker.

Part of the office accommodation was let to dockside, shipping, freighting and similar interests.

Speaking at the opening ceremony, Mr Stoker again used the style of Longfellow's Hiawatha to say:

Welcome to our brand new wigwam
Air conditioned 'gainst the hotness
Insulated 'gainst the coldness
Cosy home for eager beavers
Helicoptered on the rooftop
Totem-poled 'gainst evil spirits
Built within a virgin forest
(Will be when the trees are grown up)
Parking space for Minis — ha ha!
Perched above the fragrant water
(Five per cent is really water)
Launched with such a jolly party.

Mr Ritchie said that by courageous pioneering efforts, Manchester Liners had established the first cellular container service into Canada, had not only

Manchester Liners House at Salford Docks, opened on December 12, 1969. It has since been renamed Furness House.

strengthened the ties between two great nations but had made it possible for Canadian manufacturers attempting to break into the British market to offer their customers in Britain speedy and safe delivery of their products.

In congratulating Mr Stoker and Mr Tony Roberts, Mr Ritchie said the pioneering of container trade with Canada had been tackled with the same flair as that demonstrated by Sir Francis Drake, difficulties being surmounted with a high degree of daring and initiative.

Saying that wealth can be measured by the number of friends, Mr Ritchie assured Manchester Liners that their friends in Canada were legion.

The '70s — a Decade of Development

THE 1970s saw the container revolution producing enormous changes not only in shipping but in industrial, commercial and trading patterns, with the "box" spreading its influence to many other parts of the world in addition to the North Atlantic.

New lines came into being, heavily supported by their banks.One of these, on the American trade, was Seatrain with three very fast — and very fuel-consuming — gas turbine ships. These ships did not last very long.

Manchester Liners spread its container expertise into the Mediterranean where, from 1971 onwards the company pioneered container services to an ever-increasing number of countries.

The introduction of cellular container vessels meant that port turnround was cut from 10 or more days to a couple of days or less. There were great reductions in pilferage of and damage to cargo.

The catchment area for cargo was greatly extended. Cheap unit trains enabled cargo to be transported economically to and from distant points. For example, in Britain the rail rate from Manchester to Southampton was less than the road rate from Manchester to Birmingham.

This meant that, particularly in a relatively small country, a container port could draw cargo from the traditional hinterland of other ports. The tariff could be amended to take care of any inland figure and the cargo be taken by any line to whom the end absorption was not exorbitant.

Lines with a good base cargo could add on to that good class cargo from another area on a marginal cost basis. "Berth rights", in a sense, became outdated.

These points were, of course, debated at Conference meetings. At the end of one all-day session Mr Tony Roberts, managing director of Manchester Liners, summed matters up by saying, "It is, of course, all a matter of integrity". A spokesman for an American line retorted, inelegantly and ungrammatically, "Integrity — that's a word like Mother's Day!" Fortunately, the line he represented was one which went out of business.

Another problem was the reaction of dock labour to house-to-house container movements, for instance from a Highland distillery direct to the overseas warehouse of the importer. That kind of movement reduced port handling to a minimum.

Then there was the question of groupage, putting less than a container load into a container. This could be carried out at any inland depot, much more than at the docks where a surcharge had to be paid to the National Dock Labour Board.

Manchester Liners decided it would, none the less, be right to effect as much work as possible at the docks. A "stuffing" and "unstuffing" of containers system was established at Vere Street, Salford, just behind the container terminal.

An indication of the delicacy with which labour relations had to be handled is given by the fact that one company which, in an unguarded moment, revealed that they planned to carry out these container stuffing and unstuffing operations not at a southern docks but away from that area found themselves forced to do so for many months by transhipment across to Antwerp at very heavy cost.

The "catchment area" for cargo to and from Britain became extended over the length and breadth of Britain by explosive concurrent developments in road and rail transport, specifically or coincidentally assisting the movement of containers.

The regularity and frequency of the services enabled help in the securing of export orders, such as a £1½mn. contract for the delivery during 1971 of 22,350 tonnes of rolled steel wheel sections required by the North American vehicle industry.

Mr. W. A. L. (Tony) Roberts.

A washing machine company in Staffordshire found it possible to "drip feed" a Canadian production line with sub-assemblies and parts, only a small contingency reserve being necessary in Canada. Confectionery made in Canada arrived in Britain speedily in perfect condition, enabling sales to be increased.

Experience over the first three years demonstrated that in fact the vast majority of cargo was suitable for containerisation. About 90 per cent of the traditional cargo of Manchester Liners was moving by container. New cargo was secured by the introduction of Europex, a system giving exporters of smaller loads a completely supervised door-to-door express service from anywhere in the UK to anywhere in Canada.

Among other major export commodities to Canada were earned goods, machinery, crockery, glass, carpets, chemicals, personal effects, footwear, wines and spirits, typewriters, tea, biscuits, tools, wallpaper, cereal foods, synthetic fibre, engines, sports goods, toys, confectionery, wool, paints and electric motors.

To the United States Mid-West ports of Cleveland, Detroit, Chicago and Milwaukee went spirits, steel bars, lead ingots, diesel engines, machinery, castings, cycles, tiles, aluminium ingots, glass and sugar confectionery.

In from Canada came aluminium, asbestos, beans, canned goods, copper, ferrosilicon, iron and steel, lumber, soyameal, nickel, paper, board, newsprint, corn starch, tobacco, wood pulp and zinc; from the United States came millet, starch, dross, steel, lubricating oils, hides, sand, flour, granite and electrodes.

Airviews (M/cr) Ltd

The Port of Manchester's terminal docks at Salford.

It was during 1970, in March, that Manchester Liners, in conjunction with CP and Head Donaldson — and as inheritors of the Cairn Line — started putting vessels directly into Greenock.

Going back a little in time, it may be recalled that in the late 1960s the Donaldson Line, of Glasgow, had suffered from the arrival of the "box" in the whisky trade. They had decided that the huge investment necessary in the container field, not only for new ships but also for fleets of containers, was too heavy. The field was left for CP and ML.

The Furness Warren Line — a famous line linking Newfoundland, Nova Scotia and Boston with Liverpool — had two excellent vessels on the trade, the ***Newfoundland*** and the ***Nova Scotia.*** The Boston sector was attacked by the container, as was the Halifax trade.

Although Manchester Liners handed over their St John, New Brunswick interest, more attractive employment was found in the 1970s for these ships. Boston costs were increased by the fact that the Federal Maritime Commission pursued all the Conference Lines, the result being very time-consuming and costly. The Warren Line was out of the trade by this time.

The Bristol City Line, friends of Manchester Liners, had the same agents in Montreal — Furness Withy — and were anxious to join in a container service out of Portbury. This came to nothing, but Dart was born.

Bristol City Line then went into a consortium with Compagnie Maritime Belge and a Canadian partner, Clarke Steamships. However as Portbury was not ready this service went out of the Continent and Southampton. Later on the Bristol third share was bought by Bibby Brothers and then the Clarke share was bought by C.Y. Tung, who subsequently became the dominant partner by buying out Bibby.

The Dalgleish Line, operating to Churchill, had been started by Peter Dalgleish in the 1930s, loading full grain ships from the end of July to early October, basically two voyages. There was a period of terrible droughts and harvest in Western Canada. Peter Dalgliesh stumped the prairie provinces, followed by a Manchester Liners representative. Importers had to place their orders in May for all the year — and then found they had ordered too much. But there was a strong Western lobby at the Bay Association. Each year the ships brought in whisky for the liquor boards.

In 1968 Peter Dalgleish had led a trade mission to the area. Included in it was the managing director of Manchester Liners, selling the advantages of containers throughout the year. The attraction of the Bay route was broken. By the early 1970s both Peter and his son were tragically dead and the Dalgleish Line ended.

The Cunard Line, operating from Liverpool, became worried about the expenditure needed to run an efficient container service. They went into a consortium with Continental owners and temporarily left Liverpool.

The result was that in the early days of the container service through Montreal there was basically Manchester Liners and CP Ships. The consortium Dart Line put their ships into Halifax, combining this with the New York service.

The British lines, looking at the expenditure involved in big container ships and the tremendous back-up services required had looked to consortia, especially for long-distance trades. Furness took their interest to Australia and New Zealand, joining with the OCL container consortia.

As Manchester Liners had a big minority interest the company was excluded from this. Manchester Liners relationship with OCL was friendly — in fact pin-pointing for OCL a container base in Trafford Park which proved very successful.

The "Manchester Mercurio", one of two small containerships chartered from Spain to act as feeder ships from Montreal to Chicago.

The ***Manchester Faith*** and ***Manchester Fame*** were sold, becoming the ***Ilkon Tak*** and ***Ilkon Niki*** respectively, chartered to continue the Great Lakes service.

The ***Manchester Port, Manchester Renown, Manchester City, Manchester Miller*** and ***Manchester Progress*** were only able to carry a limited number of containers to Chicago so, in August, a feeder service from Montreal was commenced with two small container ships, the ***Manchester Rapido*** and ***Manchester Mercurio,*** chartered from Spain. These vessels took containers from Montreal on a weekly basis.

The ***Manchester Miller*** was converted in 1970 by Smith's Dock Co. Ltd. into a cellular containership and renamed ***Manchester Quest.*** The ***Manchester Progress*** was also converted for containers and ice-strengthened, becoming the ***Manchester Concept.***

The Manchester City became the ***Korean Winner***, the ***Manchester Renown*** the ***Korean Challenger***. The Yugoslavs bought the ***Manchester Port,*** which became the ***Biokovo***.

It was also in 1970 that word came that the Mediterranean lines were proposing a consortium for containers. As explained earlier, Manchester Liners had bought Prince Line loading brokers Gough and Crosthwaite, continuing services to the Mediterranean from Manchester as the Manchester Prince Line, operating small vessels to "cream" the traffic and to avoid lengthy times in port.

Although the Manchester Liners share of West Coast trade had gone down to about 5 per cent, it was a profitable percentage. It seemed clear that any consortium would operate out of Liverpool, not Manchester, and that Manchester Liners would be a very minor partner.

Visits were made by Mr Stoker and Mr D. E. Warburton, managing director of Gough and Crosthwaite, to Israel and to Cyprus to sell the container concept, in the broadest possible terms. There were difficulties because of conflicting interests but eventually these were resolved, making it possible for Manchester Liners to commence container services in the following year.

Boardroom Battle

THE year 1970 saw another development in the story of Manchester Liners. It began with what can only be described as "a row of cannons". This was a decision by Furness Withy to bid for the share capital in Manchester Liners which they did not own.

There was an interlocking directorate, Manchester Liners directors Mr James A. MaçConochie, Mr Geoffrey Murrant, Mr R. B. Stoker and Mr P.V.O. Evans (Canadian director) also being on the Furness board, Mr. MacConachie, of course, being the chairman of Furness Withy and Co. Ltd. The independent directors of Manchester Liners were Sir Leslie Roberts, Mr Tony Roberts and Mr Mark Pattinson.

It was agreed that negotiations should be carried out with the advice of the respective merchant banks of the two companies, Rae Brothers for Furness Withy and Shroder Wagg for Manchester Liners.

The merchant banks were unable to come to any agreement on a fair price. The Manchester Liners stockbrokers in Manchester, P.Q. Henriques and Company, came out strongly in the defence of Manchester Liners. They had, in fact, to appear before the Stock Exchange Council and were able to convince the council that they were not privy to special information.

Furness Withy had 42 per cent of the voting stock. A raised forecast resulted in an increase in the bid price, and at the end of a month Furness Withy gained 49.7 per cent of the shares. Their offer was extended and they then received 50.4 per cent later increased to 56 per cent.

It was a difficult period for both lots of directors. The outcome was that Manchester Liners, with a young and flourishing management team, continued as a subsidiary company to Furness Withy.

An interesting financial footnote is that from around a quarter of a million pounds profit during the 1960s, the year to the end of December 1969 showed £372,000; the next half-year

FotoFlite, Ashford, Kent

The "Manchester Challenge" at sea with a full load of containers.

£716,000 — £1,008mn. for the full year — and the following six months, to the end of December 1970, £645,000.

1971 — and a Royal Accolade

THE year 1971 was marked by vigorous expansion of container vessel services and associated interlinking activities. The ***Manchester Merit*** which had been ordered in Spain, came back from a spell in Canada. Spanish associates and friends Contemar — who were producing transhipment cargo for Canada for Manchester Liners — took her for the first two voyages as the first UK container vessel into the Mediterranean.

Early in 1971 Manchester Liners commenced container services from Manchester to the Eastern Mediterranean, to Malta, Cyprus and Israel. These services, managed by Gough and Crosthwaite, were a blend of the container expertise of Manchester Liners and the experience of Mediterranean trading, dating back to the turn of the century, by Gough and Crosthwaite as loading brokers to the long-established Prince Line.

In the beginning, Malta created a problem. When the first ship was on the way a delegation of dockers came over to re-open negotiations. The result was that the cargo was discharged at Cyprus, unstuffed and delivered to Malta break-bulk. However the difficulties were overcome and by the end of the year the Manchester Liners share of Mediterranean trade had increased from 5 per cent to 35 per cent.

In later years the container vessel services from Manchester were to be extended to Syria, Lebanon, Greece and Italy, plus a sea-land service to Iran. Sales and other functions were closely co-ordinated with those in the rest of the group. The Mediterranean services also brought the benefit of transhipment cargo through the USA and Canada — and vice-versa.

The container revolution was now firmly established — and it meant that the old concept of pier to pier rates on cargo had gone. Having to quote from the shipper's warehouse meant becoming interested and involved in road haulage.

Thomas Craig and Co. Ltd, in road haulage, container storage and repairs, had been acquired in 1970. In 1971 Manchester Liners also acquired Wardell Warehousing Ltd and Wardell Transport Ltd, of Stretton, near Warrington, and Waugh Road Services Ltd, of Benton Square Industrial Estate, near Newcastle upon Tyne. Commercial Cartage Co. Ltd, located at the East India Dock complex in London, was acquired in 1972.

This provided depots for the storage of containers and, in due course, facilities for minor repairs to containers, an activity which steadily grew in importance.

In 1971 the Queen's Award was extended, for the first time, to include invisible exports. Manchester Liners

Rodney Hall

Lord Rhodes of Saddleworth, Lord Lieutenant of Lancashire presents the Queen's Award to Mr. R. B. Stoker.

First vessel to arrive at Montreal in 1972 was the "Manchester Crusade", arriving on January 1. She is seen here at Royal Seaforth Dock, Liverpool.

gained the first Queen's Award to go to a shipping comany. Presenting the award in September of that year the Lord Lieutenant, Lord Rhodes, said: "You at Manchester Liners have a way of blazing a trail".

All the vessels of Manchester Liners flew the Queen's Award flag.

By the end of the year Manchester Liners was operating the four 12,000 tons deadweight "Challenge" class container vessels, the 10,000 tons deadweight ***Manchester Quest*** and the 4,500 tons deadweight ***Manchester Merit.*** Other container ships, such as the two Great Lakes feeder vessels based at Montreal, were on charter.

In addition, orders had been placed with British yards for two further container vessels of 4,490 tons deadweight for delivery in 1973, plus orders worth £10mn. for two improved "Challenge" class container vessels for delivery in 1975.

At this period, looking into the future, Manchester Liners became involved with a cargo airship project, an idea revived in the light of new materials and technology to extend container traffic into the areas with poor or non-existent road or rail facilities.

A subsidiary company, Cargo Airships Ltd, was created on a fifty-fifty basis with airship enthusiast and publicist Max Rynish. Feasibility and design studies were commenced in the UK and Canada, an aeronautical engineer was hired and patents were later taken out. The project certainly attracted a great deal of publicity. However although there certainly seemed a future for the right design for the craft, it was subsequently decided to withdraw from this project.

The year 1972 started with a first, when Capt Denis Millard took the ***Manchester Crusade*** into Montreal on January 1, the first vessel to arrive. He was presented with the symbolic Gold Cane. The vessel was the fourth of the "Challenge" class container ships to go into service.

A second gantry crane, of 35 tonnes capacity, was in action at the Manchester Container Terminal. The terminal's water frontage had been increased to 850 ft. and could now berth two vessels.

Labour troubles continued both in Canada and Manchester, a dock strike lasting for nine weeks in Montreal closing the container terminal there for that period. There was also a four-week UK national dock strike.

In September, the formal interline agreement between Manchester Liners and CP Air was signed on board the ***Manchester Crusade*** complementing that already signed between the company and Air Canada.

Despite all problems, the company was still expanding and still looking for fresh developments associated with containers. The Lakes feeder service had been augmented by the Spanish vessel ***Fortuna*** and delivery was also taken of the vessel ***Frontier,*** which was suitable for the Mediterranean trade.

In January 1973 Mr Philip K. Gorick was appointed as chief executive of Manchester Liners operations in North America and a director of Manchester Liners (Canada) Ltd of which Mr P.V.O. (Peter) Evans was President.

It had also been decided to broaden the company's base. Instead of operating two ships a week out of Manchester, which was liable to strike disruption, there would be one out of Manchester and one out of Felixstowe and Rotterdam, commencing in April.

The Rotterdam - Felixstowe - Montreal service opened new opportunities for Canadian and European manufacturers at a period marked by Britain's entry into the European Economic Community. The feeder container services from Montreal were also of interest to Continental importers and exporters.

It was evident that the Rotterdam service, while very promising, would take some time to get into real profitability. After two years with poor results, completely outside the company's control, Mr Stoker went to Montreal where he saw Mr Ian Sinclair, chairman of CP and suggested that after some 70 years it was possibly time to work together rather than as competitors.

CP ships were losing money on their service out of Liverpool so this approach was received favourably. Negotiations took place through the summer between Mr Tony Roberts and CP. In January 1974 Manchester Liners withdrew the Felixstowe - Rotterdam - Montreal service and CP withdrew its Liverpool - Glasgow - Montreal service.

In mid-1973 delivery was taken of the ***Manchester Vigour*** and ***Manchester Zeal,*** built under cover at Appledore. These were small general purpose vessels which could be used on the Mediterranean, the North Atlantic or be chartered. In fact during the next two years they were variously on charter to Australia, to the American Gulf and then on the North Atlantic to the USA for a year.

To cater for cargo which would not go into containers Golden Cross Line, under the management of Mr. Tony Lowry, went into action.

Industrial peace in 1973, for a change, produced a profit of £645,000 instead of the loss of £516,000 for the comparative period in the previous year. The result in the peaceful year of 1974 can be judged by the fact that the company made £6.1mn.

The 75th anniversary of the company was in 1973. Congratulations came in from Mr Michael Heseltine, Minister for Aerospace and Shipping; and in Canada from the Rt. Hon. Pierre Elliott Trudeau, Prime Minister and his Minister of Transport, the Rt. Hon. Jean Marchant; the Hon. Alastair Gillespie, Canadian Minister of Industry, Trade and Commerce; from Mr J. H. Warren, Canadian High Commissioner in the UK; Mr Ward Cornell, Agent General for Ontario, and Mr Jean Fournier, Agent General for Quebec, both based in the UK; from the Lord Mayor of Manchester, Alderman Edward Grant; the Mayor of Montreal, M. Jean Drapeau; and Mayor Richard J. Daley, Chicago.

Manchester Dry Docks Ltd, was acquired by Manchester Liners Ltd. in 1974.

There were, of course, a great many other congratulations and good wishes from shippers, all of which showed something of the esteem in which Manchester Liners was held.

In January 1974 Manchester Liners established its own offices in Montreal, Toronto and Winnipeg, the majority of the staff of former general agents Furness Withy becoming Manchester Liners employees. Capt Clive W. Meadowcroft, based in Manchester, and Mr Philip Gorick, based in Montreal, were appointed directors of Manchester Liners Ltd.

Capt Meadowcroft, holder of an extra master's certificate, joined the company in 1968, serving in various commercial roles in the UK, Europe and Canada and being especially concerned with diversification policies.

Mr Gorick, who continued as chief executive of the company's operations in North America, joined Furness Withy in 1950, serving in the Far East, New York and London. In 1964 he was appointed personal assistant to Sir Errington Keville, chairman of Furness Withy; in 1966 a manager of Furness Withy, London; in 1970 chairman of the USA Board and later director of the North American Divisional Board and President of the Furness Withy USA organisation.

Mr. Peter Evans left the ML board to make way for Mr. Gorick, and Mr. Stoker paid a special tribute to Mr. Evans for the way he had looked after the Canadian affairs of Manchester Liners.

Further companies were acquired, Manchester Dry Docks Ltd., in 1974, and also E. Wilcox and Co. (Chains) Ltd., the latter specialising in manufacturing, repairing and merchanting lifting tackle. Manchester Dry Docks owned three dry docks and a small

Skyfotos Ltd., New Romney, Kent

Delivered in 1975, the "Manchester Reward" was one of two sister ships. The "Manchester Renown" was the other.

pontoon dock in the Port of Manchester.

It was really necessary to have dry docks to keep the fleet going. By putting the dry docks together with the marine engineering company Morrell Mills, which had been acquired in 1968, the means existed not only to maintain ships but also to repair and refurbish containers in conjunction with Container Workshops Ltd.

To ensure the better utilisation of containers a data link was installed between Manchester and Montreal. The computer contained full details of the location of all 12,000 containers on both sides of the Atlantic. Every container movement was entered within hours. Visual display units were employed for both entering data and to permit instant interrogation of the computer in real time.

Again, Manchester Liners were leading — the only container company on the North Atlantic at the time to have both a transatlantic data link and VDUs for the purpose of container utilisation control.

At the beginning of 1975 the Mediterranean container services were extended to Greece, the ***Manchester Mercurio*** making the first voyage, sailing on January 18.

Further developments in the Mediterranean were also in hand. Following intensive investigations into ways and means of providing a new container route to Iran from the UK the decision was made to pioneer a service by sea to the Turkish port of Iskenderun and then by road across Turkey to Iran, crossing only one land frontier.

The Medliners-Iran service was inaugurated in July 1975 with the sailing of the vessel ***Manchester Falcon*** from Manchester.

Arrangements had been made for a 25-tonne crane in Iskenderun and for a fleet of vehicles able to take containers on a four-day journey to Teheran, passing near to Mount Ararat, supposed to be the resting place of Noah's Ark.

Another development was the formation of an equal joint company with container manufacturers Adamson Hatchett to produce housing units to container dimensions — and with the portability of containers. The company was named Manchester Adamson. However as in the case of Cargo

Picture Coverage Ltd.

German-registered, but a Manchester Liner nonetheless. The "Manchester Falcon" in the Ship Canal, approaching Latchford Locks.

Airships, ·it eventually proved that a fifty-fifty company was not really the way to success.

Two new vessels, the ***Manchester Reward*** and ***Manchester Renown,*** were delivered during the summer. Within a short time the contribution from these vessels, operating on charter in the Far East, helped the company to weather the storms of strikes

Container terminal, No. 9 Dock, Manchester, with the "Manchester Concorde" alongside.

in Canada and Manchester.

The year 1975 also saw the appointment of Furness Withy director Mr. Brian Shaw to the board of Manchester Liners. Sir Leslie Roberts, father of Mr. Tony Roberts, decided not to seek re-election to the Manchester Liners board, on which he had served since 1947. Mr. Shaw — who was subsequently to become chairman of Furness Withy — was invited to succeed him on the ML board.

Sir Leslie had retired in 1971 as chairman of the Manchester Ship Canal Company, being appointed honorary president. His shipping experience included executive service on the boards of the Leyland Line, Royal Mail Lines and The Pacific Steam Navigation Company.

The year 1975 ended on a high note with a new record — the 100th crossing of the North Atlantic by the ***Manchester Challenge.*** Mr. Nick Beshwaty, on behalf of the Montreal Harbour Authority, presented the master of the ship Capt. James Illingworth, with an Eskimo carving to mark the occasion.

The ***Manchester Concorde*** was not far behind, completing her 100 voyages when she arrived at Manchester on February 18, 1976 under the command of Capt. Eric Askew.

During her seven years and 100 voyages the ***Manchester Challenge*** carried 95,000 containers across the North Atlantic to and from Montreal, which added up to 1,438,590 tonnes. She had logged 553,819 miles, the equivalent of a return trip to the moon.

BID FOR MANCHESTER LINERS

IN the autumn of 1974 there was another partial take-over of Manchester Liners, Furness increasing their holding to 61.6 per cent. This had been brought about to some degree by the activities of Eurocanadian Shipholdings Ltd (ECS) otherwise known as Cast.

Since the end of the 1960s Cast had been chartering vessels to carry bulk loads of steel westbound and copper matte eastbound, to and from the St. Lawrence and Antwerp.

Mr. F. Narby, one of the founders of the company — a Canadian citizen

with previous experience of shipping in Egypt, London and in Canada, was an astute and capable charterer. He saw the possibility of putting better class cargo above his bulk carryings.

This was the way in which Sea-Land had started. Manchester Liners had done the same thing before containers by putting liner board from Savannah on top of bulk phosphate from Tampa.

By getting a contract for the carriage of asbestos, Cast was in the simple container business with little capital expenditure. The ships, boxes and mobile cranes could be hired.

Cast started to buy Manchester Liners shares and put in a bid for those not owned by Furness Withy, which was a minority of 44 per cent. Furness decided to try to buy the Manchester-held shares to keep them in friendly hands, to bring their holdings up to 75 per cent. However stockbrokers in Manchester had a millionaire client who bought up all the shares on offer and held them for the highest bidder. Clearly, it was not possible to tell local friends to sell to Furness Withy below the market price.

At the time Lord Beeching, chairman of Furness Withy, was in Germany. The guide lines could not be altered. At first the holding of Cast hardly changed. Furness raised their stakes from 56 per cent to nearly 62 per cent with around 30 per cent of the shares held by the "third man."

Cast then raised the ante from about 110 pence to 155 pence becoming the owners of 37.6 per cent of the equity, with only 0.8 per cent still left as private shareholders. Naturally, the Stock Exchange held an inquiry into the share dealings of the Manchester Liners directors, who were completely exonerated of any wrong doing.

As Cast had been cutting rates on the Canadian-Continental trade and evidently had ambitions about UK trade, Manchester Liners felt that with a large shareholding they would have an interest in Manchester Liners being profitable.

Furness held a meeting with Cast but could not progress any ideas further — so the situation developed that Manchester Liners had majority and minority shareholders who were not talking to each other.

ECS had been buying Furness Withy ordinary shares since June 1974 — and then further efforts to influence Manchester Liners through Furness Withy were begun. Cast, with help from its bankers, built up the stake in Furness Withy, assisted by the forced sale of tanker owner Reksten's shares, acquiring 425,000 by August 1974.

By mid-July 1975 ECS had acquired nearly 2.5 mn Furness Withy shares, Mr. Narby stating that this was to pursue his aim of getting control of Manchester Liners.

Some small sales were subsequently made, reducing the ECS holding in Furness Withy to 2,376,500. However in August, Mr. Narby struck a bargain with Hambros Bank Ltd (Hambros) for the purchase of about 19 per cent of the Furness Withy equity.

In October 1975 Canadian National Railways (CNR) joined Cast by taking an 18 per cent share, Dr. R. A. Bandeen, president and chief executive officer of CNR, becoming a director. This no doubt helped Cast to get further credit.

On November 28, 1975 the Department of Prices and Consumer Protection referred the matter to the Monoplies and Mergers Commission which then set up a group, under the chairmanship of Mr. J. G. Le Quesne QC, to carry out the inquiry. During the period of the inquiry ECS made further purchases of Furness Withy ordineary shares. By June 10, 1976 ECS held 6,673,960 ordinary shares, representing 24.9 per cent of the issued ordinary capital of Furness Withy.

The hearings of the commission were held during the summer of 1976 under the title "Eurocanadian Shipholdings Ltd and Furness, Withy and Company Ltd and Manchester Liners Ltd."

Manchester Liners, during the hearings, learned for the first time of the ECS objective: to combine the non-Conference service from Antwerp in a three-cornered service via Liverpool to Montreal, using the two new 1,000 TEU Manchester Liners ships, when they were available, and aiming eventually at bigger ships.

The 1,000 TEU container vessels had been ordered by Manchester Liners from Smith's Dock Co. Ltd., for delivery in 1977 — the ***Manchester Vanguard*** and ***Manchester Venture.*** The 1,000 TEU capacity was decided on the best advice of the Furness chartering department as the size to fill a gap in the market.

An independent study by the Marine Transport Centre, Liverpool, confirmed that if both sizes of ships — that is around 560 TEU and 1,200 TEU — were full, there was a saving of about 16 per cent in favour of the bigger ship. However there were many problems. Furness Withy were very unhappy about Cast having board representation as they were also ship operators on the worldwide market. The other Conference operators were also unhappy at a joint office and service run by a line non-Conference to the Continent and Conference to the UK.

CP Ships, especially, having gone out of Liverpool, were in a threatening mood to break up the agreement reached in 1974 with Manchester Liners. This would have resulted in a big reduction in the cargoes of Manchester Liners.

British shippers said that Manchester Liners was the only wholly British line in the UK/Canada trade, that its management was readily accessible and exceptionally effective in support of British interestes, and that the company was too important to be under foreign control.

The chairman of the North Atlantic Shippers' Association said that "while

Skyfotos Ltd., New Romney, Kent

Containership "Manchester Vanguard", capable of carrying 1,000 TEUs.

nobody is perfect ML is as good a shipping line both as an operator and a Conference member as shippers can realistically hope to see." Many other bodies put in reports, speaking well of Manchester Liners.

The commission, in its report published in October 1976, ruled that the proposed merger was against the public interest, stating: "We consider that Manchester Liners is an effective company; in particular it has an impressive record of enterprise and successful innovation.

"We received not a single criticism from Manchester Liners customers of the way in which it conducts its business and got positive testimony of the quality of the service which it provides."

Cast was by no means pleased with this judgement and began to put their vessels from Antwerp into Liverpool in order to reduce the carryings of Manchester Liners. However the Liverpool labour went on strike and so Cast pulled out from Liverpool with a view to putting this competitive UK service out of Avonmouth.

When their vessel approached Avonmouth the ancillary workers went out on strike. Cast pulled away from Avonmouth, decided they had had enough of UK labour and that their future lay in operations from Antwerp which would be serviced by feeders from UK ports. The situation arose where Glasgow cargo went from Leith to Antwerp and other cargo going across from London or Harwich.

The story of Manchester Liners was to be dictated for the next few years by the efforts of Cast to increase its carryings.

The Second Half of the Seventies

IN 1976 Manchester Liners received another Royal tribute — the presentation of a second Queen's Export Award, an unparalleled achievement. The first Award, made in 1971, recognised the company's work in pioneering Britain's deep-sea cellular container vessel services; the second the earnings brought in from the charter market.

The company, seeking new challenges, then decided that worldwide trading opportunities could be created by the chartering out of cellular container ships. Four vessels, built in Britain for this market, brought valuable export revenue. Two further vessels were on order from Smith's Dock, Middlesbrough, at an approximate total delivered price of £18 mn. During the previous three years the company had increased overseas earnings by almost £15 mn.

The company's container vessels were trading across the Atlantic to the American continent, in the St. Lawrence Seaway, the Great Lakes, the Mediterranean and Middle East, to the Continent and in the Far East.

When the award was presented in August by the Lord Lieutenant, Mr. William A. Downward, he praised the company's container developments, saying "Advances such as this come from co-operation at all levels."

As he spoke, moves were afoot to capitalise on containerisation skills by further broadening the base of the company. Two directors, Mr. Mark Pattinson and Capt. Clive Meadowcroft, went out to look at possibilities in the Middle East, Mr. Pattinson chosen because of his financial expertise, Capt. Meadowcroft of his technical "know-how."

After one false start in the Gulf, negotiations began with the Alireza family in Jeddah for the setting up of a joint company, The Marine Transport International Company Ltd. Less than three years after its formation, the company was to become the world's largest non-shipping line port management operator.

Among other highlights of 1976: the shipping of around three million teabags for the Montreal Olympics and the 50th voyage to Chicago by Capt. H. M. Bunker, master of the Lakes feeder vessel ***Kathleen.***

August saw the retirement of Mr. D. E. Warburton, managing director of Gough and Crosthwaite, followed by the appointment of co-director Mr. R. A. H. (Ray) Farrer as executive manager of the Mediterranean Division of Manchester Liners.

A sad event in the middle of the year, was the death of Sir Leslie Roberts, CBE, former chairman of the Manchester Ship Canal Company and director of Manchester Liners.

On January 1, 1977, the symbolic Gold Cane for the first vessel into Montreal went to Capt. William Hancock, master of the Canadian-registered ***Sir John Crosbie,*** on charter to the Golden Cross Line.

Mr. Brian Shaw became managing director of Furness Withy, and Mr. Tony Roberts was appointed to the Furness Withy board, the ***Manchester Vigour*** and ***Manchester Zeal*** went on to Mediterranean service, the new 946 TEU vessel ***Manchester Vanguard*** made her maiden voyage and the sister vessel ***Manchester Venture*** was launched by Mrs. Bryanne Alireza, wife of Sheikh Faisal A. Alireza.

Marine Transport International, 64 per cent owned by the Alireza organisation, and 36 per cent by Manchester Liners, was contracted by the Saudi Ports Authority, under the leadership of Dr. Fayez I. Badr, president and chairman of the board, to operate and manage a container berth at Jeddah on behalf of and in conjunction with the authority and the Jeddah Port administration.

The chairman of MTI was Sheikh Youssef M. Alireza; Vice-Chairman and Chief Executive, Sheikh Fahd M. Alireza; President, Mr. Mark Pattinson, Directors, Sheikh Faisal A. Alireza and Capt. Clive Meadowcroft.

Between March and December the whole 30-acre site was fitted out with a Liebherr 90-tonne gantry crane, straddle carriers and fork-lift trucks, with Manchester Adamson "Marco" units for the housing complex.

The berth, number 16, was so successful that it was equipped with a second gantry crane and, in the following year, MTI were awarded the contracts to manage and operate two further container berths at Jeddah, numbers 35 and 36.

In order to expand MTI's operations elsewhere a crane was sent out to India to commence container berth services in Bombay. However there was great difficulty in getting money out of India so that this scheme had less attraction than another new container terminal of which the management, later on, was offered.

This terminal at Khor Fakkah in Sharjah, United Arab Emirates was just outside the Hormuz Strait mouth of the Arabian Gulf, strategically situated not only for sending cargo through the Gulf States without having to go into the Arabian Gulf but also for transporting cargo to or from India.

Manchester Liners was also given the opportunity to acquire one line and go into partnership with another to that part of the world but it was decided to concentrate on handling boxes at the terminals.

A supplement published by International Freighting Weekly at the start of 1978 bore the headline "Manchester Liners — born in 1898 and still going strong."

There were two reasons for celebration. It was not only the 80th birthday year of the company but also the year in which Manchester Liners completed a decade of fully-cellular transatlantic container vessel services.

The year began with another first when Capt. Eric Askew took the ***Manchester Concorde*** into Montreal on New Year's Day, to collect the Gold Cane. It was a double celebration for him, too, for a few days later his daughter, living in Toronto, produced a

The "Manchester Venture" at Royal Seaforth container terminal, Liverpool.

baby girl. However it was also a year again of unofficial strikes.

The decision was made to operate the North Atlantic service from Liverpool, the Mediterranean services continuing from Manchester. At this period the charter market began to go sour with the result that the ***Manchester Renown*** and ***Manchester Reward*** came home from the Far East. The ***Manchester Challenge*** and ***Manchester Courage*** were sold.

The £ started to move higher, affecting the company's dollar freight — and a four week lorry strike played havoc with carryings. There was world-wide depression, resulting in Governments subsidising and in fact almost giving away ships.

The rise in the £ had also made the return on the chartering out of vessels, particularly the ***Manchester Vanguard*** and ***Manchester Venture*** much lower than expected. Although there was demand for them, it was on the basis of 50 per cent of the return which had been predicted and depreciation on loan interest could not be earned, an especially serious matter with the ***Manchester Vanguard.***

The background to this was the fact that shipowners had been encouraged to place orders by the concession of being credited with 100 per cent depreciation in the first year. This meant that if they had a big tax bill they received a refund — but also meant that in future years there was not the benefit of taking the year's depreciation off the tax bill.

Assets and borrowing powers were increased, but there was a tread mill effect, to continue building new ships.

The company's tax experts had produced a scheme — rather in advance of its time — whereby through a complex financial structure, Pilkington Brothers, who paid a great deal of tax, bought 75 per cent of the Golden Cross Line, the line which ordered the ***Manchester Vanguard.***

However the expected £8 mn. refund, on the basis of which the ship was ordered, did not arrive for the new owners. The Revenue found some chinks in the agreement. The case went up to the House of Lords in 1982, who found for the Revenue.

There was employment for lawyers but not for British shipbuilders whom the legislation was designed to assist.

In August 1978 Capt. Dennis Millard retired, his place as commodore being taken by Capt. Alan Cookson. Both had been seafarers since boyhood.

STRIKES - IN BRITAIN AND CANADA

STRIKES which disrupted the 1960s did not end with with the start of the 1970s. Unofficial strikes took place at Manchester Docks despite the saving of Prince Line services for Manchester and the fact that all possible was done at the start of containerisation to safeguard jobs at the docks. The problem continued intermittently throughout the decade, and was a major factor in the decline of the Port of Manchester.

Direct employers of labour can establish close and trusting relationships with their employees. However Manchester Liners did not employ the dockers — and nor did the company which paid them, the Manchester Ship Canal Company.

The dockers were in the army of the National Dock Labour Board, formed as a result of a social experiment designed to give greater security and a bigger say to the workmen. The men were allocated to employers — at Manchester the Manchester Ship Canal — who collected a levy on behalf of the Dock Labour Board.

On the local board were representatives of the Transport and General Workers' Union (T&GWU), the "white" union — and employers, including shipowners, on a 50-50 basis. This meant that the union officials, instead of exclusively loooking after the interests of a member, could also be judge and jury on a disciplinary panel.

The root of the problem went back to the 1967 national dock strike. After that strike, the dockers were all "decasualised", that is, they not only had a continuous job but a job for life.

Lord Brown, of Glacier Metals, who was an idealistic Socialist, and Mr. Frank Cousins, of the T&GWU, produced this wide-ranging scheme under the umbrella of the National Dock Labour Board.

The board, although operating on levies from the employers, fostered loyalty to itself through clubs and events such as races or rowing competitions. But in fact it formed a wedge between the employers and the men, preventing the loyaltly and understanding which good employers are able to create.

The job guarantee was given at a time when every type of cargo-handling — bulk, pallets and containers — was becoming less labour intensive. This "fairyland" situation had a great deal to do with the gradual self-destruction of the jobs of dockers.

In 1971 a series of first one-day, then two and three-day strikes commenced at Manchester. No notice was given, and the result was that customers kept their cargoes away. It was a real boost to new emerging competitor lines.

The strikes ended in June, but it took a long time to re-establish confidence. Some of the cargo which Manchester Liners had developed from the Continent through the Port of Manchester disappeared for ever.

The problem went deeper. The "blue" union — London stevedores — established an autonomous branch in Manchester. They had been kicked out of Trades Union Congress for poaching, so they were not recognised.

The T&GWU forbade the Manchester Ship Canal Company to recognise the "blue" union on pain of refusing to allow ships into the port. Unofficial meetings were called on the "croft" by the "blue" union. They wanted higher rates to be negotiated by the Port Modernisation Committee — on which they were not represented, but on which the T&GWU had 50 per cent representation.

A report in the "Manchester Evening News" stated: "Only those lucky enough to work at the container terminal get a good day's pay".

As the "meat in the sandwich", Manchester Liners, from a profit of £716,000, turned in a loss of £440,000.

During 1972 there was further disruption in Montreal in May and June. Due to the unit train operation from Halifax, Nova Scotia, there was much less traffic going through the Port of Montreal. With no arrangements to cushion the dockers, they went on strike — and hurt the very people who were giving them the most work.

At the end of nine weeks, the Canadian Federal Government ordered the dockers back to work. In the meantime, the vessels had to go into Halifax or straight up into the Lakes. When they got back to the UK there was a national dock strike for four weeks which was only settled by the well-known Jones/Alderton Report. These two strikes cost Manchester Liners £1½mn. but the year's loss was only £111,000.

In 1976 there were again strikes in the St. Lawrence from the end of March to May and unofficial strikes until July.

Manchester Liners fought hard behind the scenes to prevent nationalisation of the main British ports, believing the result would be a bonanza for Antwerp and a disaster for Britain.

Looking back on this period is interesting. On January 18 1984 the "Financial Times", in an article on the Transport and General Workers' Union, stated: "The T&GWU used to bestride Britain's trade unions like a Colossus. Its voice was heard everywhere.

"The General Secretaries became Government Ministers, its ideas became Acts of Parliament. At the height of its influences in the 1970s Mr. Jack Jones was seen as the most powerful man in Britain".

Comment by the authors: "But at local level, with a closed shop, the officials were impotent to influence their members. It was the weakness, rather than the strength of the union which was so disastrous. They could not control their own militants — and that was our tragedy."

Retirement of "Mr. Manchester Liners"

In 1979 there were top-level changes in the board structures of Furness Withy and Manchester Liners. Mr. Brian P. Shaw, managing director of Furness Withy, succeeded Sir James Steel at the end of June, taking over the joint roles of chairman and managing director.

Mr. R. B. Stoker retired from the Furness Withy board at the same time. Mr. T. R. Pulley, of Furness Withy, joined Mr. Shaw on the Manchester Liners board.

Mr. Geoffrey Murrant resigned as deputy chairman of Furness Withy and retired from the board of Manchester Liners. His father, Sir Ernest Murrant, served Furness Withy as chairman of Manchester Liners from 1944 to 1959.

In July, having reached the age of 65, Mr. Stoker retired as chairman of Manchester Liners, being succeeded by Mr. Tony Roberts, who continued as managing director.

Changing Times

THE closing years of the 1970s brought many influences to bear on the world-wide development of containerisation and the fortunes of shipping companies.

On the North Atlantic the activities of non-Conference carriers in a fierce rate-cutting war were a major factor in producing headlines such as "Who will survive?", "Steaming into the red" and "Rates battle of the Atlantic."

Another headline, in the noted shipping daily "Journal of Commerce" made clever use of the names of ML vessels. Referring to the departure of two of the original containerships from the Montreal service and the arrival of two larger ML ships on the route, the headline read: "Challenge with Courage brings Reward and Renown."

The impact of the Common Market was making itself felt, with the emphasis on getting into Europe, bringing the South East coast into greater prominence.

Rate-cutting was biting deep. As an example, a loyal North of England shipper with Manchester Liners received a lower quote for Canada by transhipment through Antwerp. When Manchester Liners then reduced rates to compete, there were complaints from Continental shippers. It was a disturbing development.

These were difficult times for cargo liner trades, affecting Furness Withy and Manchester Liners, not to mention other major carriers. Counter measures were taken by Furness Withy the group's wholly-owned shipowning operations being integrated into one company, Furness Withy (Shipping) Ltd., as from May 1, 1979. Appointed chairman, Mr. J. E. Keville assumed responsibility for all the activities previously carried on by the general shipping and bulk shipping divisions.

The "Manchester Challenge" goes down "the big ditch" from Manchester.

The "Crown Prince" joined the Manchester Prince Line in 1979.

The ***Manchester Vanguard*** and ***Manchester Venture,*** operating under the names of ***Keelung*** and ***Marseille*** respectively, were chartered out for a whole year. The ***Frontier*** and ***Manchester Courage*** were sold.

The ***Crown Prince*** and ***Royal Prince*** were among five new ships delivered to the Furness Withy Group.

In the Mediterranean a rationalisation of services to Arab areas in the Middle East was effected, Prince Line's share of the trade being covered by slot charters in association with Manchester Liners.

Surveying the 1979 scene from his new chairman and managing director viewpoint, Mr. Tony Roberts said: "It is well known to the management of shipping companies that some part of their operations will be adversely affected by matters outside their control, e.g. industrial disputes, currency fluctuations, vagaries of the charter market, a slow working of UK ports through lack of available equipment and inability speedily to receive and deliver container transport to and from the terminals.

"In 1979 we had the misfortune to be adversely affected in every sector of our United Kingdom trading activities, resulting in a serious loss.

"During the first two months of the year the road haulage strike and 'secondary picketing' resulted in the blockading of all UK ports and brought the fleet to a standstill.

"This militant action by the labour unions also took a toll upon the trade of our road haulage companies and the marine engineering group.

"Equally disappointing was the depressed world charter scene for those of our containerships made available on the market as the result of the lack of activity from the UK. These ships, which had been trading profitably, were chartered out together with our regular ships for the charter market, in a weak dollar-earning currency.

When the blockade ended, urgent steps were taken to get our North Atlantic and Mediterranean trades flowing again.

"The road haulage companies quickly regained their profitability but the engineering group continued with work unrest and against severe competition from the nationalised ship repair yards who were bidding at depressed rates for the limited business available.

"Losses continued and eventually the nettle had to be grasped. Manchester Dry Docks Ltd., Morrell Mills and Co. Ltd. and Container Workshops Ltd., were placed in creditors' voluntary liquidation, E. Wilcox and Co., (Chains) Ltd., was sold and James Walker and Sons (Shipping) Ltd., was closed down.

"These were old and respected companies but painful decisions were necessary to get us back into shape."

Quantifying the effects of industrial disputes on profits, Mr. Roberts said the loss on sales on the liner services during the road haulage strike resulted in a shortfall in contribution to profits of more than £2mn. The engineering companies, before closure in August 1979, had lost in excess of 10.5mn.

Because of the depressed market and weak US dollar, the ships out on charter, while covering their operating costs, failed to meet the total cost of their depreciation.

"The 1979 loss put a severe strain on the cash flow," said Mr. Roberts. "Current high loan interest charges for a company such as ours — which employs assets of a value many times in excess of an historically narrow based capital structure — erode the profits."

The Medliners-Iran sea-road service was affected by increasing chaos in Iran caused by anti-Shah factions.

On a brighter note, the Marine Transport International Co. Ltd., in which Manchester Liners had a 36 per cent share, was doing well in managing and operating container terminals at Jeddah, Saudi Arabia, and at Khor Fakkan, Sharjah.

The Golden Cross Line subsidiary made news by carrying the biggest lift ever from the Port of Manchester in a conventional ship, a 210-tonne stator core for Sundance hydro-electric power scheme in Canada.

Not to be left out of the picture, the heavy-lift capabilities of the North Atlantic and Mediterranean services were also in the news. A power station boiler weighing 116 long tonnes was shipped from Erie, Pennsylvania to the Middle East. It was carried from Erie to Montreal on the ML feeder containership ***Kathleen,*** transferred at Montreal to the ***Manchester Concorde*** and at Liverpool to the ***Manchester Faith*** for the final leg of the journey, in a total sailing time of 19 days.

In the Mediterranean, against a background of overtonnaging and rate-cutting, the United Kingdom/Mediterranean Container Conference was born. Original members of the new Conference included Manchester Liners, Adriatica di Navigazione, Contship, P&O Strath, Prince Line and Ellerman City Liners, covering ports in Malta, Greece, Cyprus, Lebanon and Southern Turkey plus through carriage to hinterland destinations.

Under New Management

MANY of the headlines in 1979 and 1980 were in the financial pages, relating the last chapters of the shares battle between Eurocanadian Shipholdings Ltd (Cast), Furness Withy and Manchester Liners, in the wake of the 1976 Report of the Monopolies Commission.

Typical in 1979 were "The thrust and parry at Furness Withy", "Narby attacks in FW battle", "No love match", "Struggle for power" and "Furness repels boarders."

In early 1980 the headline writers had to cope with another factor — the arrival on the scene of the C.Y. Tung Group. Headlines in February and March read: "Tung wants Furness" and "C.Y. Tung bid to clinch Furness." On February 14 the business staff of the "Manchester Evening News" wrote: "Last night Furness collected a surprise takeover bid from one of the most fascinating shipping men in the world, C.Y. Tung, of Hong Kong."

On March 17, 1980 the board of Furness Withy and Co. Ltd., unanimously recommended to shareholders an offer of 420p per share by Orient Overseas Containers (Holdings) Ltd. The offer, made by Kenwake Holdings Ltd., a wholly-owned subsidiary company of OOC(H)L — part of the C.Y. Tung Group, of Hong Kong — was successful.

As a result of acquiring the majority of the issued capital of Furness Withy and Co. Ltd., OOC(H)L had, of course, also acquired the 61.6 per cent equity of Manchester Liners held by Furness Withy.

The 37.6 per cent ordinary shareholding by Eurocanadian (Cast) in Manchester Liners was purchased by Rendish Investment Ltd., a member of the C.Y. Tung Group.

The man who built up Orient Overseas, Chao Yung (C.Y.) Tung, the second largest shipowner in Hong Kong, was in his late 60s at the time. His interests included the Europe/Far East container trade through the fast-growing Orient Overseas Container Line; a stake in the Dart Containerline operating between UK/Continent and North America; membership through OOCL of a Far East/Australia container consortium; and a Middle East service by OOCL.

In the mid-70s he handed over the day-to-day running of the business to his sons Chee Hwa (C.H.) Tung (cargo

A chartered ship running on the Mediterranean service was the "Fulmar", later "Manchester Fulmar".

operations) and Chee Chen (C.C.) Tung, North American operations.

Assurances were given that Furness Withy would continue to be developed as a major British group, retaining the British character of the company and management in Britain, with vessels sailing under the British flag and manned by British officers and crews.

Mr. C. H. Tung, chairman and managing director of Orient Overseas Container (Holdings) Ltd. Morley I. Cho and Mr. C. C. Tung, both OOC(H)L directors, joined the Furness Withy board as non-executive directors.

The other seven Furness Withy board members were: Mr. Brian Shaw, chairman and managing director; Sir Ralph Bateman, deputy chairman (former chairman, Turner and Newall); Mr. John Gawne, executive director (chairman of The Pacific Steam Navigation Company); Mr. John Houlder (chairman, Houlder Offshore); Mr. John Keville (chief executive, Furness Withy Shipping); Mr. Tom Pulley, finance director; Mr. Tony Roberts (chairman and managing director, Manchester Liners).

Mr. Shaw, who joined the board of OOC(H)L, said Furness Withy looked forward to working in a much larger group with world-wide interests and potential.

"We shall be glad to concentrate on the future of the business without having to spend half the time stopping to look over our shoulder," he said. "It is an exciting and challenging prospect."

Commented Mr. Roberts: "The C.Y. Tung Group, together with Furness Withy, will be helping the company to continue developing its container service on the North Atlantic route as well as other activities — but, as usual, our future will rest on our own efforts."

The start of the Eighties

MANY forces affecting shipping were reaching a climax when Mr. Roberts took over the helm of Manchester Liners.

The three years from 1980 to 1983 will undoubtedly go down in shipping history as a period when the older order underwent rapid change, yielding place to new, never to be the same again.

The stark background of the latter half of the 1970s was that overheads had escalated practically beyond control. Fuel prices increased dramatically. The cost of oil reached 50 per cent of a ship's operating costs. Seamen's wages had continued to rise considerably. At the same time, worldwide recession was deepening.

All these factors affected the North Atlantic in the 1980s. The Cast Line — plus, in due course, the break-away Sofati Line — continued cut-throat rate cutting despite falling cargo tonnages, especially Westbound. Too many slots were chasing too little cargo. The Atlantic Ocean was being described as a "battleground" and a "bloodbath."

Another difficulty for Manchester Liners, was the problems of chartering out surplus containerships for which there was little demand. And, as ever, there were strikes, particularly the seamen's strike at the beginning of 1981, lasting until mid-February.

As losses mounted, great shipping lines plunged into the red. Famous names like Hansa, Farrell and Seatrain headed for the bottom or limped off the Atlantic sea lanes.

During 1980, in the closing stages of the Furness Withy and Manchester Liners share activities of Cast Line, financial dealings continued until the take-over of Furness Withy and Manchester Liners by the Tung Group.

The year 1980 started in drearily familiar style as far as Manchester Liners were concerned. Liverpool Docks were closed for two weeks while the dockers supported a totally unrelated strike of steel workers causing losses to the North Atlantic and Mediterranean services. Mr. Roberts wondered openly when strikers would

Container operations on the "Manchester Fulmar".

realise that the consequence of their actions was to jeopardise their employment and that of others.

All was done to maintain regular and efficient North Atlantic and Mediterranean services, while boardroom meetings were held to discuss the far-reaching measures needed to ensure survival. As a matter of policy and necessity it seemed clear that lines with complementary interests would have to join together, forgetting differences, to gain the strength of big groupings.

Despite upheavals in Iran and the Lebanon, compared with the North Atlantic the Mediterranean seemed comparitively stable. The Mediterranean vessels operated with regularity to most destinations. When it was not possible to go to Beirut the vessels went to Lattakia and Tartous in Syria and, for a time, to Tripoli. Boxes were travelling to Iraq via Iskenderun.

The Floralies International Garden Festival was held in Montreal from May to September 1980. The ***Manchester Renown*** transported a complete British garden for the festival in a 40 ft container, winning praise from Dick Balfour, former chief accountant of the Bank of England, chairman of the co-ordinating committee for the British garden.

Writing to Mr. Roberts, Mr. Balfour said, "You must be proud to be chairman of such an efficient company with such helpful and cheerful staff."

Film-maker Brian Vaughton travelled to Montreal and on by feeder vessel into the Great Lakes, then sailed out again from Manchester to the Mediterranean, producing a half-hour documentary film about the container services of Manchester Liners.

Bill Martin was appointed owner's representative of Manchester Liners, centrally-based in Cyprus.

In August the Med Division opened a Manchester-Naples service (later transferred to Salerno), bringing the total of countries served to seven, sailing regularly to nine Mediterranean ports.

On October 30, Manchester Liners held a reception at the new Container Terminal in Chicago — Iroquois Landing — to commemorate the arrival of the first container vessel, the motorship ***Liberta.***

In Sharjah, Marine Transportation International (UAE) Ltd., built a floating ro-ro berth at the Khor Fakkan Container Terminal, officially opend by His Highness Sheikh Saqr Bin Mohammed al-Qasimi, able to handle two ro-ro vessels simultaneously. Conflict which had broken out between Iraq and Iran served to highlight the strategic location of Khor Fakkan, outside the vital Strait of Hormuz, entrance to the Gulf.

On December 31 Capt. Eric Askew retired. He had joined the company after being twice torpedoed during the war, served on the ***Manchester Progress*** as third officer, obtained his master's certificate in 1947, and took over the ***Manchester Progress*** in 1956. In 1978 he gained the Gold Cane, the **Manchester Concorde** being first of the New Year into Montreal.

Share dealings continued. In October the Tung Group and Compagnie Maritime Belge (CMB) acquired the Dart shares held by the old-established Bibby Line, of Liverpool.

In 1981 the seamen's strike brought services to a standstill, meaning that the year started with a group loss of $1\frac{1}{2}$ mn.

During that year, Westbound freight revenue per container for Manchester Liners was a mere 4 per cent over the level for 1979, quite insuffficent to cover the percentage increase in overhead costs. There were special problems in Lebanon as fighting continually flared. Life was not easy for Manchester Liners — nor for many other operators.

Action was taken by the "big three" North Atlantic operators servicing Canada to stem the tide. In the Spring, Manchester Liners, as members of Furness Withy (Shipping) Ltd., Dart Containerline (Canada) and Canadian Pacific announced plans for a new co-ordinated weekly container service, operating from Walton Container Terminal, a subsidiary of OOC(H)L Felixstowe, to the Racine Container Terminal Montreal to commence in August 1981.

Mr. Roberts, deputy chairman of Furness Withy (Shipping), chairman and managing director of Manchester Liners, explained: "The whole concept of this new venture is that the three companies will continue exactly as before by way of marketing and selling with a view to retaining and hopefully expanding their share of the market, each providing their usual back-up services such as documentation, container control and inland transportation."

Instead of the three companies providing their own North Atlantic ships of medium size they would utilise four large container vessels, each company providing one ship and sharing in the fourth. The vessels, to be named ***Manchester Challenge, Dart Europe, CP Ambassador*** and ***Canadian Explorer*** would provide a regularly weekly service, Eastbound and Westbound, sailing not only from Felixstowe, but also from Hamburg, Antwerp and Le Havre.

In preparation for the new service, Dart vessels were being re-fitted to carry 1,800 TEU and ice-strengthened, said Mr. Roberts.

The new St. Lawrence Co-ordinated Service (SLCS) from Felixstowe would mean withdrawing Manchester Liners services from Liverpool and Greenock to Montreal. It also means that while providing the same amount of capacity only four vessels would be required instead of eleven.

The company opened a branch office at Felixstowe, Mr. Sam Wall moving from Manchester to become manager, with Mr. Robert Barnacle also going there as his assistant.

"With the current background conditions on the North Atlantic Manchester Liners had a very uncertain future because of the size of its vessels and the restricted market of the UK", said Mr. Roberts.

"The integrated service enables ML to be an important member of the newest and strongest 'big battalion' on the North Atlantic."

The calls being made in Germany, Belgium and France by the new service meant that Manchester Liners had to return to the Continent for cargo. Mr. Derek Spanton was appointed general manager — Continent, and no time was lost in setting up a strong network of continental general agencies.

Representatives of Jokelson and Handtsaem, of France; Phs. Van Ommeren NV, of the Netherlands and Belgium; and Aug. Bolten, Wm. Miller's Nachfolger, of Germany, met in Manchester with UK directors and executives, plus ML staff from Canada and the USA, to discuss combined operations.

Willem D. Passenier was appointed ML owner's representative — Continental Europe, based in Antwerp. A considerable linguist, he was fluent in English, French, German and Dutch, with a working knowledge of Portuguese and Spanish.

The SLCS Service commenced in August, initially with the sailing of the ***Manchester Vanguard*** from Felixstowe and the ***Manchester Concorde*** from Montreal.

The second ***Manchester Challenge,*** captained by John McKay, was the first of the four 1,800 TEU vessels to join the service. She arrived at Walton Container Terminal, Felixstowe from Hamburg and Antwerp at the beginning of October, going to Le Havre and Montreal carrying cargo from the Continent and the UK for Canada and the US Mid-West. The new North Atlantic era had begun.

In November, almost 12 years to the day after the start of Britain's containership services by the first ***Manchester Challenge*** the second ***Manchester Challenge*** was in the news, carrying the 2,000,000th container into the Port of Montreal. The port gave a reception to mark the occasion.

In the Middle East the MTI container berths at Jeddah were thriving — but Khor Fakkan was in temporary difficulties after the closing of Mideast Cargo Services.

Changes were also afoot on the Mediterranean front. Mr. John Keville, chairman of Furness Withy (Shipping) saw that when Furness Withy acquired Manchester Liners it was an opportune moment to bring together ML and Prince Line under one management.

Board responsibility for the company's interests in the Mediterranean was given to Mr. C. A. (Chris) Skelton, director of Furness Withy (Shipping) and Manchester Liners. Mr. R. A. H. (Ray) Farrer was appointed manager — Mediterranean Trades.

Mr. David Penny, a director of Prince Line, moved to Manchester to assist Mr. Farrer, and Mr. Arthur Whalley, one of ML's most experienced salesmen, became sales manager — Mediterranean.

* * *

DEATH OF C.Y. TUNG

THE road haulage subsidiary companies were also fighting the problems of the national recession, with its consequent drop in business and squeezing of rates, together with the fact that Manchester Liners ceased to operate through Liverpool and Greenock.

The road haulage services of the Wardell Services Group at Stretton, Warrington, were particularly badly hit, making it necessary to close these by the end of the year. However plans were in hand there to double the Wardell container repair capacity — and for Commercial Container Transport to open a new transport and container depot at Dagenham, Essex, moving from East India Dock.

Studies had also been taking place in the knowledge of the fact that all Furness Withy (Shipping) major trade routes would be primarily container trades in the near future.

The decision was made to integrate documentation, sales, marketing and transport functions in a Liner Services Division, with Mr. Roberts assuming overall responsibility for the division, based in Manchester.

Key appointments were: Mr. Tim Alcock, executive manager; Mr. John Killick, manager — sales and marketing; Mr. David Brown, container operations co-ordinator.

Said Mr. John Keville, chairman and managing director of Furness Withy (Shipping): "The creations of the división will have far-reaching implications across the company. I believe this is a vital step in our development and one which I know will continue significantly to the company's future."

In April 1982 came the death of C. Y. Tung. Although small in stature, he was one of the biggest men on the world shipping scene. Born in Shanghai, he started his career in coastal shipping. By the age of 24 he was vice-president of the Tientsin Ship Owners' Association.

In 1948 he moved to Hong Kong, starting operations with one 10,000-ton vessel. From these beginnings he developed a fleet which, at the time of his death, numbered some 140 ships totalling about 11mn. tons.

In later years he had tended to hand over much of the day-to-day control of the C. Y. Tung Group to his eldest son, C. H. Tung, who played a leading part in the 1980 negotiations resulting in Furness Withy becoming part of the Tung Group.

Integration continued of complementary aspects of Manchester Liners, Prince Line, The Pacific Steam Navigation Company, Royal Mail Lines and Houlder Line, all members of Furness Withy (Shipping) Ltd.

These lines, together with associated companies, served over 50 ports in the North, Central and South America, Europe, the Mediterranean and North Africa.

In January 1982 Royal Mail Lines, as partners in the four-company Streamline consortium, had commenced multi-purpose ro-ro services from

Liverpool to the Caribbean and East Coast Central America. As loading brokers and UK general agents for the Central America Service (CAS), Royal Mail also served Panama and the West Coast of Central America.

Royal Mail and Houlder provided container and conventional services to East Coast South America and the River Plate.

The Pacific Steam Navigation Company, nearing 150 years of trading to the West Coast of South America, was building up — as the British partner in the nine-line Eurosal consortium — towards the introduction of fully-cellular container vessel services to Colombia (Pacific), Ecuador, Peru and Chile, to commence in 1984.

In 1982 PSNC were operating a container service to Bermuda, plus associated and joint container/break bulk services to these countries as well as acting as UK agents and loading brokers for Linabol and Transnave services.

Prince Line, in addition to container services, provided conventional sailings to North African destinations.

The vast range of services available from these Furness Withy (Shipping) lines, with the strength of a large group plus the individuality, experience and personal attention on which they had been built up, was marketed in various ways, including a large stand at an international freight exhibition held in Manchester.

By the end of the year directors and top executives of PSNC, Royal Mail Lines, Houlder Line and Prince Line moved to the former Manchester Liners House, re-named Furness House, at the Port of Manchester, while still maintaining bases in London and Liverpool.

During June the Mediterranean Division had notched up its 20,000th container to Malta, carried by the ***Manchester Faith***. The cargo: grocery provisions.

In the same month, the container vessel ***Royal Prince*** was involved in the rescue of British subjects from war-torn Lebanon, picking them up at Junieh, a small port North of Beirut and taking them to Cyprus. Services to Beirut were temporarily suspended, being resumed as soon as conditions permitted, just over two months later.

On the North Atlantic, Manchester Liners won praise from a Yorkshire company, shipping its 1,500th container to Montreal, practically one a week since ML started fully-cellular container vessel services in 1968.

A youthful-looking Mr Neville Hall, executive manager — North Atlantic, retired in October after 45 years of service, to be succeeded by Mr John Edmonds.

At the year's end another cut-rate operation appeared on the North Atlantic scene, despite a continuing drop in the volume of trade. Breaking away from the Cast Line, a group of management employees set up Sofati Container Lines to trade between the Continent, UK and Canada, using cheap chartered vessels.

Commented Mr Roberts: "The situation is volatile and the whole complexion can change at short notice. With all lines studying their unsatisfactory figures we have to believe that changes will take place sooner or later.

"Maximum pressure is on to attack all costs. Fortunately, the three members of SLCS are the strongest and most effective companies within the trade".

There was another "retirement" in December 1982 — that of "Manchester Liners News", the company's house journal, first published in March 1961.

David Attenborough, a man who had served ML all his working life, continued to serve in his retirement when he was appointed editor. In the last issue, Volume 22, number 3, he chronicled the journal's highlights as allegiance was transferred to "The

Mr. Ray Farrer, executive manager Mediterranean trades, Furness Withy (Shipping) Ltd.

Log", the Furness Withy house magazine. Thanks were recorded to Mrs Freda Hunt, "ML News" editorial secretary, and all contributors.

There were more vast changes throughout 1983, the year which saw Cast itself in considerable financial difficulties. The year was to close with North Atlantic shippers, who had never had it so good, facing rate increases — and a slight gleam on the horizon as world trade showed signs of picking up. As 1984 dawned the Conference lines, fingers crossed, were hoping it signalled the end of the doldrums.

The first change to be rung in by the 1983 New Year was in Canada. From January 1 Mr. Philip Gorick and his staff in Canada and the United States Mid-West became Manchester Liners Services (Canada) Inc., a separate company within the Tung Group, which also incorporated Eckert Overseas Agencies (Canada) Ltd.

Mr. Gorick and his team were to act as general agents for the Furness Withy North Atlantic service and as agents in Canada for OOCL, previously handled by Dart Containerline, Canada.

The scene also changed in the United States Mid-West when, from March 1, Manchester Liners appointed Seapac — also a Tung company — as sub-agents in place of Kerr Steamships, a company which had carried out an excellent job for Liners over many years.

The pattern continued of rationalising services by combining operations to meet competition, this time affecting the Mediterranean. In July Manchester Liners/Prince Line, as members of Furness Withy (Shipping) Ltd., together with Ellerman City Liners and Zim Israel Navigation formed a joint venture named Combined Container Services. The plan: to provide two services, one operating from the North West and Dublin and the other from the South East.

Ellesmere Port was chosen in the North West, Victoria Deep Water Terminal, London, in the South East.

Mr. Chris Skelton, Furness Withy director, Mediterranean Trades, explained: "We are sad to be leaving the Manchester terminal docks after such a long and happy relationship. The move is in no way a reflection on their service.

"Ellerman City and Zim already operated from Ellesmere Port, so it was logical that Manchester Liners would be the company to switch terminals."

Mr. David Penny was appointed line manager of the Manchester Prince Line container services and Mr. Tony Lowry as manager of the line's conventional services to North Africa.

On the North Atlantic, the Conference carriers had come firmly to the conclusion that, as Mr. Roberts put it, the "rot had to stop". It was announced that some rates would be going up from November and others from the beginning of January 1984.

"One might have referred to this as 'an increase in freight rates', but

Skyfotos Ltd., New Romney, Kent

The "Manchester Vanguard" with a full load of containers.

perhaps the more accurate description is that a start is being made for 'recovery of rate reductions', he said.

"It is hoped that a major contributing factor is the formation of Cast (1983) Ltd., incorporating both Sofati and Cast, which were fighting each other as well as the Conference lines prior to Eurocanadian (Shipholdings) Ltd. and Cast (North America) being placed in the hands of the Receiver.

"Cast (1983) Ltd. has now been formed and will continue to be a major carrier in the trade. It is anticipated that, like the other lines, serious steps must be taken to pull up its freight rates from the present disastrous levels."

Cast, in fact, announced substantial rate increases effective from November 1, 1983. Also looming on the horizon, to come into effect in 1984, was a change in the management of the St. Lawrence Co-ordinated Service, meaning that it would be operated by two companies instead of three.

In addition, the Dart Containerline service between Europe and the US East Coast, was to be wholly owned by the Tung Group by January 1, 1984, following an agreement reached with Canadian Pacific and Compagnie Maritime Belge.At the time of the announcement, October 1983, the Tung Group, CP Ships and CMB had a one-third interest each in the service.

It was stressed that there would be no interruption in the regular weekly service from Southampton (Mayflower Container Terminal) and European ports to New York, Charleston, Norfolk and Baltimore.

On the St. Lawrence route, Manchester Liners, CP Ships and CMB would continue the joint operation between Europe and Montreal, using the same vessels.

CP Ships and CMB would however act jointly with a new company — The Canada Line — working in partnership with Manchester Liners. Dart and Manchester Liners were also to form a new company for the Canadian trade.

Commented Mr. Stoker: "Manchester Liners, in different form, managed to survive one of the most concentrated assaults, backed with seemingly unlimited bank money, to which any company has been exposed.

"The fact that it has done so is due in very great measure to Mr. Roberts, as chairman and chief executive from

A Manchester container liner pushing through ice in the St. Lawrence.

1979, who was able to keep the support of his colleagues not only in Furness Withy itself but in their new owners, the C.Y. Tung Group".

PERILS — AND RESCUES AT SEA

THROUGH two world wars and intervening years of "peace" the vessels and crews of Manchester Liners have been involved in their share of hazards and deeds of heroism. The 25 years from 1958 to 1983 were no exception.

During the early 1960s the ***Manchester Progress*** and ***Manchester Faith*** played a vital part in rescuing passengers and crew of a

Constellation airliner which had ditched in mid-Atlantic, the former acting as a relay station for the rescue operation while the latter a far smaller vessel, picked up some of the survivors from rafts, 48 out of a total of 76 being saved.

In August 1967 the ***Manchester Exporter*** was some 450 miles off Northern Ireland when there was a fire on board, apparently caused by chemicals in the cargo. In the after hold were drums of sodium peroxide and one had apparently spilled some of the contents. The chemical reaction on making contact with organic matter — whether rope, dunnage or skeleton case — was to cause spontaneous combustion. The after hatch was blown off.

Capt. L. Taylor and his crew fought the heat, fumes and smoke from 05.10 hours until 13.50 hours. Some of the crew were in the poop and had to reach the centre castle by means of the tunnel escape. Unfortunately, the exertion was too much for one of the engine staff, Mr. McVeigh, who suffered a heart attack. The ***Manchester Merchant*** and ***Manchester Faith*** were among the vessels standing by.

Finally, the ***Manchester Exporter*** was able to proceed under her own steam to Belfast and the 12 passengers who were on board were flown on to their destinations.

A year later a similar fate befell the ***Manchester Miller*** in New York when loading chemicals. Before the fire was put out Capt. A. G. Rowlands found himself host to 200 firemen, 42 appliances, two fire tenders and attendant tugs.

With water at 500 lbs per sq. in. from eight-inch hoses and holes cut in the side of the ship to put out the fire and with the ship settling on the bottom at a seven-degree list, there is little doubt that if it happened at sea the ***Manchester Miller*** would have been a total wreck.

View of the bridge from the bridge. A Manchester Liner approaching the Quebec Bridge over the St. Lawrence.

Greenock container terminal with the "Manchester Venture" alongside.

However the ship, with almost the whole of her after accommodation destroyed, was taken to Todd's Shipyard, temporary repairs were carried out and, with a smaller crew living in the passenger accommodation, the vessel came home via the Azores for permanent repairs.

The crew quarters were not replaced, the crew continuing to use cabins built for passengers. It meant that the vessel provided superb comfort for the engineers.

In 1969 a fire developed in the cargo of the ***Manchester Merchant*** bound from the USA. On board was a full cargo and a number of passengers.

The fire, reported at 02.00 hours in No. 3 hatch, forward of the funnel and aft of the bridge, seemed to be developing in bales of nylon, the cause — although never completely established — possibly being due to friction of steel bands on the nylon bales.

The flames were soon 6ft high accompanied by a very nasty smell. The crew, wearing smoke helmets and breathing apparatus, played hoses on the flames. The fire was very close to oil fuel and preparations were made to abandon ship but, after seven hours, the blaze was extinguished, thanks to the fine efforts of Capt. D. S. Millard, his officers and crew, and the vessel sailed to Halifax.

The nuclear ship ***Savannah*** — the first atomic merchant ship of her kind — and the ***Rotadyke*** had answered distress calls, the ***Savannah*** standing by until the end of the emergency.

In December 1974 a "Mayday" call from the Canadian motorship ***Jennifer*** off Sheboygan, Wisconsin, in Lake Michigan, sent the ***Fortuna*** on a course 30 miles across the lake to help. The ***Jennifer's*** cargo of steel had shifted, causing her to heel over 40 deg. gradually righting to a 25 deg. starboard list, and the vessel was rolling heavily in 10 ft. waves.

The wind was blowing at gale force out of the North East over Lake Michigan on the night of November 30, when the ***Fortuna*** sailed from Burns Harbour, bound for Cleveland with a cargo of containers.

The "Manchester Reward", chartered out for Far Eastern service as the "Asian Reward."

Capt. H. M. Bunker reported later that the vessel, fighting through short, steep and nasty waters, was "ducking and weaving like a heavyweight boxer" At 23.00 hours the distress call from the ***Jennifer*** was received.

By 01.10 hours the ***Fortuna*** had reached the ***Jennifer*** which was still heading North East at six knots although her starboard bulwark was under water and heavy spray was sweeping the decks. Slowly, her list increased. Just after 04.00 hours a US Coast Guard helicopter took off four crew members.

The ***Fortuna*** fired a rocket line but it parted. At 05.00 hours the ***Jennifer's*** captain decided to abandon ship. The ***Fortuna,*** the ***Venus*** and a Spanish freighter ***Monte Zaraya*** all closed in. A lifeboat pulled clear of the stricken ship which settled by the head and then plunged down.

The ***Fortuna*** drifted to the lifeboat which had 11 men aboard. They scrambled up nets and the pilot ladder. One man fell back into the boat. The ***Fortuna*** launched one of her own boats so that the man could climb into it and be hoisted aboard on the davits.

US Rear Admiral J. S. Gracey commended the ***Fortuna's*** captain and crew for their expeditious actions, responsible for saving the 11 men. None of the ***Jennifer's*** crew was lost.

On August 21, 1978, the 17,385 ton ***Seatrain Trenton*** (ex-***Manchester Vanguard),*** out on charter, not only resuced two people from the stranded yacht ***Desert Princess*** but also saved the yacht, earning a letter of commendation from the US Coast Guard.

The container ship was en route between Tokyo and Los Angeles when Capt. P. D. Cullen was told of a distress call that a 26 ft. yacht adrift with two people on board with little food and water remaining. Contact was made with a Starmaster US Coast Guard reconnaissance aircraft which reported that the ***Desert Princess*** was only about 40 miles away.

Course was altered to the yacht's indicated position and, as the sun was setting, radar contact was made at a distance of $7\frac{1}{2}$ miles. The yacht, on passage from Hawaii to San Diego, had been drifting for four days with smashed steering gear.

The husband and wife crew on the yacht, from Arizona, were brought on board the ***Seatrain Trenton*** and then the yacht itself was lifted on to the big ship's deck.

Rescue assistance which not only hit the headlines but was also featured on television news bulletins was given in 1982 by the new ***Manchester Challenge*** when she went to the aid of the Greek tanker ***Victory.***

The ***Victory,*** on her way from Florida to Liverpool with a cargo of molasses, had broken in half in a Force 12 gale when 800 miles off Land's End. The ***Manchester Challenge*** en route from Montreal to Felixstowe, received the ***Victory***'s distress call at 00.29 GMT on Friday, February 12. Ship's master Capt. John McKay, still on duty because of the weather, said: "We were about 95 miles away. Because of the weather we couldn't head straight for the ***Victory*** but we reached her by mid-afternoon. It took us 12 hours.

"The sight was amazing. Only 100 ft of the 500 ft. long 12,480 ton ***Victory*** remained afloat — the bridge, radio room, crew's quarters, engine room and a few feet of deck. Huddled on the hulk, which was "bobbing about like a cork" were half of the crew including the captain.

Loading a 40 ft. container into the cellular hold of a Manchester Liners North Atlantic container vessel.

Built in Spain in 1972, the "Frontier" later became the "Manchester Frontier" on the Mediterranean service.

A Belgian cargo ship the ***Potomac*** had been trying, without success, to get a line aboard. She pulled away for the ***Manchester Challenge*** to try. Third mate Colin Eke fired one of the vessel's four rockets and got a hit the first time. The Greeks collected the line, but because of the weather, it parted. A second shot missed. The third shot was successful.

Said Capt. McKay: "We wanted them to heave in the line so that we could pass a stronger one, attach a raft, into which they could put half a dozen men and we could heave them back.

"They were reluctant to leave the ship and get into the water. We could understand their thinking. After all, 13 fellows in the bow section had abandoned ship and not been seen in the mountainous seas. They wanted helicopters.

"By the time we got the second line aboard it was towards 17.00 hours and getting dark. We knew the Dutch Navy would not get there until daylight and their helicopter couldn't be in action till then.

"But they were right, weren't they? The maxim is to hang on to the biggest thing afloat and that's just what they did."

As night fell, Falmouth rescue headquarters in Cornwall asked two ships to stand by. The ***Potomac*** proceeded, the ***Manchester Challenge*** and the ***Dusseldorf Express*** stood off a short distance away, the former keeping on their searchlight to provide a bit of comfort.

Around midnight the Greeks asked the ***Manchester Challenge*** to come back. The hulk was listing badly. Apparently three men had taken to the water, not to be seen again.

... fired our last rocket — and missed ... said Capt. McKay. "But the list became stabilised and the weather was improving. It was down to gale force."

In daylight the Dutch frigate ***Van Speyk*** arrived. A Lynx helicopter from the frigate managed to airlift the remaining 17 men — one unfortunately found to be dead when brought on board the frigate — and the Greek captain, last to leave his ship.

After a search for survivors — none being found — the ***Manchester Challenge*** went on to Felixstowe. Capt. McKay had been hard at it without sleep for 48 hours, not only directing operations but also, when pressures eased, talking to journalists by radio telephone, explaining what was happening. His account was broadcast on TV networks, synchronised with amazing film shots of the scene taken from an RAF Nimrod aircraft.

Thanks were received from the Greek Government, from the owners of the ***Victory***, from Falmouth rescue headquarters — and the ***Victory***'s Greek captain.

Cast and Clouts

THE Eurocanadian Cast company's efforts to take over Manchester Liners and/or Furness Withy, rate-cutting and other activities, caused considerable upheaval and change on the North Atlantic shipping scene during the 1970s and into the 1980s.

Both as a participant until his retirement in 1979 and from the "sidelines", the writer had a special interest. This is his review of the "Cast period" and some of its far-reaching effects:

The Cast company commenced operations at the end of the 1960s by chartering vessels to carry bulk loads to and from the St. Lawrence and Antwerp. One of the great ambitions of every successful charterer is to become a shipowner for at least part of his activities in case there should be a dramatic rise in chartering rates.

Perhaps one year in 10 rates become too high for the charterer to pay and, therefore, he is unable to carry his cargo without a very big loss.

In the mid-70s Cast were extending more and more into the USA which represented 45 per cent of their carryings in 1975. The company was changing from one with cheap, low overheads, carrying one box type to nearby hinterlands, into a more widespread liner operation, with increased overheads and vulnerability.

Cast had stated to the Mergers and Monopolies Commission that "the present range and size of their (Manchester Liners) operations offer little scope for cost reduction and if it (ML) did no more then continue its present operations its cost advantages over its competitors would tend to disappear".

Putting a fine quality captive trade on to larger vessels would have been beneficial to Cast. It was why they had their eye on Manchester Liners.

If this was not possible — and the commission's recommendations meant it was not — there was only one way for Cast to increase carrying and this was by extending their geographical sphere of operations.

What was not brought out in the commission's findings was that although the big ship had an advantage over the smaller ship carrying from A to B, containerisation meant that the ship was only a small part of the operation.

Moving container cargo from, say, Southern Europe, means a smaller return because of the length of time the container is out of operation plus possibly the cost of positioning with an empty leg.

In the same way, if operations are extended into, say, the American Mid-West, the further you go the more imbalance there might be and the more you are on marginal costings. Really, the most important thing is a balance of the trade.

If, for example, container cargo is taken to Minneapolis it will take a long time and probably have to go from one railway to another. Having arrived at Minneapolis, the container will be discharged and, if there is no cargo waiting there, the container will probably have to go back to a depot in Chicago, be examined and cleaned and possibly stay there for a month, dependent on the number of containers there, until needed by a shipper in, say, Kansas City. This means another "dead leg".

The further operations are extended, the more one is becoming dependent on marginal cargo. It is interesting to see how these factors develop.

In selling the Manchester Liners and Furness Withy shares Cast probably received a profit on the two transactions of well over £10 mn. They then really "went to town", with the aid of their enthusiastic bankers, particularly the Royal Bank of Canada, with whom their shareholders had a good connection.

First they bought seven OBO carriers worth 108 mn. dollars from a subsidiary of P & O. Then they ordered two 105,000-tonne deadweight combination carriers from South Korea and contracted in Yugoslavia, no doubt on very desirable terms, for six 70,000-tonne deadweight container/bulk vessels with a capacity of nearly 1,500 boxes, with extensive credits from the Yugoslavs.

Around this time the US Seatrain Lines got into trouble. Early in 1980 they sold their Pacific operation to C.Y. Tung and then achieved the distinction of selling their North Atlantic trade to Trans Freight Lines, part of the TNT group of Australia, and at the same time sold their offices to Cast.

This produced certain legal animosities and did not make for good relations with TFL, who were a non-Conference carrier in the USA and who had reckoned they were going to double their carryings from Seatrain.

There is no doubt that Cast's management thought that Cast would get a considerable slice of this business by taking over the offices.

Seatrain had had a service calling at the Continent and Greenock for the American ports, using very expensive gas turbine vessels. When these vessels were withdrawn for re-

The West German flag container ship "Lindo" was chartered as a feeder ship in the Great Lakes area.

engining, Seatrain in fact had chartered the ***Manchester Renown*** and ***Manchester Reward*** from Manchester Liners.

However basically the 20 Seatrain offices with their 200 staff and 1,000 40 ft. containers were for the USA trade. Cast had traditionally been a 20 ft. container operator.

I have already given my views on going into the American Mid-West — and quite obviously Cast were going deeper and deeper into the American interior. There is a Rudyard Kipling quotation, "The bleating of the kid excites the tiger".

Manchester Liners, as an American trading line having roots in the Mid-West, took in a limited amount of selected Mid-West cargo but were careful not to exasperate American "tigers" by being too aggressive, taking an unfair share of their cargo. This would, particularly, be the case with another non-Conference line out of the USA — which TFL was.

Cast were considerably increasing their capacity but they were also increasing their overheads: they were getting into more and more marginal business and, at the same time, inviting the American lines to take competitive action to force down the rates — action which was taken in the next year or so, with great success.

In November 1980 the "Financial Times" in an article entitled "On the crest of a wave" pointed out the tremendous growth of three million tonnes. Having got up to around 90,000 containers, the new intended vessels were to double that capacity.

The question, of course, was how they were to be filled. They could only obviously be filled by more and more marginal cargc, which would rather detract from the advantages of lower unit costs.

Not only had Seatrain gone under the but Farrell Lines had gone, so had the small independent Menav — and Cargo Lines, to whom we had also chartered the ***Manchester Zeal*** and ***Manchester Vigour,*** renamed ***Cargo Zeal*** and ***Cargo Vigour,*** in 1976.

The question raised by the pundits of the "Financial Times" was whether the Cast group was growing too fast for safety.

Cast increased their activities in the UK and bought a 322-TEU vessel from Spain which they called the ***Cast Trout*** to operate between Ipswich and Antwerp, and had plans to increase the capacity calculating they would be able to bring 45,000 TEUs in a year to and from the UK — more than their carryings in earlier days from Antwerp.

All this UK cargo would have to be transported, of course, to Ipswich, loaded, discharged and carried to their berth, which meant that the net return was less than if it had been obtained locally.

By February 1982 the "Financial Times" was reporting, "Mr. Narby hoists the storm cones".

Dart, one of the original lines serving Canada through Halifax on their way to New York, was operating directly into Montreal as partners in the new St. Lawrence Co-ordinated Service. This was a very serious matter for Halifax which owed its entire container operations to Canadian National Railways — CNR.

CNR is a Canadian Crown Corporation and, therefore, subject to political pressures. The Nova Scotia Government felt it was wrong for CNR to be so heavily involved with Cast. These pressures mounted, particularly when Cast, having bought what might be called "tramp" vessels, found that they were running them at a loss.

CNR had an option for increasing their shareholding in Cast but decided they would not do so and in fact started distancing themselves from Cast.

The "Financial Times," on February 18, 1982, reported that Dr. Bandeen,

President of CNR, had resigned from Cast — although there was no connection with these premises but it did mean that this connection was lost — and not only that, they got a court injuction to stop Cast transferring assets to Bermuda.

Two days later the "FT" reported that problems had arisen regarding the big container/bulk carriers being built in South Korea costing 60 mn. dollars each but which, because of the slump, were now worth only 30 mn dollars apiece.

However, Cast managed to make arrangements for re-financing but it was quite evident they were having difficulty in meeting their payments on these enormous commitments. A week later "Fairplay" announced that Cast were proposing to sell 50 per cent of the container operation.

The year 1982 was evidently one of financial problems for Cast. On April 24 it was announced in the "FT" that Cast were raising 200 mn. dollars by selling ships and other assets and leasing them back to the Royal Bank of Canada and the Bank of Montreal.

CNR were given an option to acquire 75 per cent of the container business but this option was not exercised. The banks made 40 mn. dollars available for two years, while another bank, the Chemical Bank of the USA, took over three vessels and cancelled 40 mn. dollars.

Cast also announced that it was withdrawing unilaterally from the rate war on the North Atlantic and started to talk to Conference.

By September, 37 of the Cast personnel decided that they would, with the assistance of a Montreal industrial organisation, start up an opposition line, Sofati Container Shipping Ltd. Interestingly enough, this was planned to start with three ships, the size of the original Manchester Liners vessels, to go from Antwerp, and call in at London and Montreal.

Quite obviously, with these smaller vessels they could not afford to go out for the larger marginal costing business all over the Continent and, therefore — in direct competition with Cast as another independent, they were going directly for what might be called the "natural" cargo to and from Cast's profitable hinterland. Cast then gave up negotiations with the Conference.

In 1982 exports from Canada to Europe were down by 15.6 per cent and imports down by 10 per cent. Cast's five new buildings had an annual capacity of 150,000 TEUs, or 60 per cent of the trade — at a time when there was more capacity available than container cargo to fill them.

The rough seas had become infinitely more rough for Cast. Not only was Sofati hurting, but the new St. Lawrence Co-ordinated Service operated by Manchester Liners, CP Ships and Dart was hitting back. The American lines, in particular Sea-Land through American ports, and Trans Freight Lines, were quoting intermodal rates into the American hinterland. The Sofati Line claimed to be carrying around 30,000 containers a year.

The Conference too, was meeting all the rates it needed to, so much so that "Fairplay" in March 1983, described them as "being those of the mid-70s and lunacy with 1983 costs."

But the Conference lines were prepared to match rates rather than have their business taken away.

Sofati was claiming to be breaking even on its plain and simple chartering operation while Cast said they were breaking even on operating costs but not making any contribution to interest charges nor capital charges — but these, of course, were desperately needed.

By July 1983 the Banks and the Receiver moved into Cast. The Banks set up Cast (1983) Ltd., to manage the vessels they had financed.

Just at that time, the first of the new super container/bulk vessels, the ***Cast***

Caribou and the ***Cast Polar Bear,*** were due for re-delivery after dry docking. "Fairplay" reported, on July 14, 1983, that they had been taken over by Yugoslav owners and chartered out to Cast (1983) Ltd.

In the year ended March 31, 1975, with about 39,000 containers, Cast made nearly £8 mn., half coming, of course, from the charter market. In 1982, with about 100,000 containers, it "made a positive cash flow."

"Fairplay" announced in January 1983 that in the 12 months to March 31, 1982, there was a loss of 35 mn. dollars and, overall, a loss of 52 mn. dollars — and this was likely to be worse in 1983.

By the end of June "Fairplay" was reporting that the Royal Bank of Canada was exposed to the tune of 275 mn. dollars. This made the £60 mn. owed by the Reksten Group, who had a very substantial record of good earnings to Hambros, look peanuts.

Following examination by the Receivers, two things happened — the first was for Cast to buy Sofati and the second was to apply to the Conference. The wheel had come full circle.

During the financial problems of 1982 the "FT" — on February 18, quoted Mr. Narby as saying he was "an innocent by-stander, clipped by a passing car."

What is certain is that a great many innocent people suffered tremendous hardship as a result of the activities of Cast.

* * *

EARLY in 1985 just three vessels bore the "Manchester" prefix to carry on the tradition of "Liners." They are the ***Manchester Challenge*** (ex-***Dart America)*** (30,817 gross tons) on the North Atlantic and the ***Manchester Crown*** (ex-***Crown Prince)*** and the German-flag ***Manchester Trader*** (ex-***Lamara),*** the latter chartered for the Mediterranean service from Ellesmere Port.

No Manchester Liners reach the terminal docks at Manchester, and the upper-section of the once-busy Ship Canal above Runcorn faces the possibility of closure.

The "Manchester Faith" and "Lindo" berthed together at Manchester container terminal.

Montreal Container Terminal, where 1,000 containers can be stored under a huge snow shed.

He had been chief in the steamer ***Knutsford,*** chartered for two years to carry coal from Australia to Shanghai. Each day the ship would consume 20 tons of coal and 10 tons of water. So each night the hatches were opened and 30 tons of the purest Pacific water would enrich the coal — so the vessel would arrive at the same draft at which she had left. The coal was paid for on arrival.

The master, the owner's cousin, could afford to leave the sea early!

* * *

THE Furness Line had for many years operated from London and Hull to Montreal but by the very early 1930s this service had folded up and Ellerman's Wilson Line plugged the Hull gap with a three-weekly service.

Their first ship to Montreal, the ***Consuelo***, took the Gold Cane, but there was very little westbound cargo and Ellermans stopped their service in 1961.

They shared agents in Montreal with McLean Kennedy, who were also agents for the privately-owned Head Line, of Belfast. Before the war they took parcels of grain to Irish ports, getting a premium for such ports as Londonderry. Then, during the war, they were directed also into Liverpool and stayed there after the war.

They built faster ships like the ***Ramore Head*** fitted with turbines and believed (probably wrongly) to be a first cousin of the Manchester Liners ships. Being faster, they were able to make a deal with Canadian Pacific to load on their berth out of Liverpool.

When the containers came the ***Inishowen Head*** was converted for them and sailed on the Liverpool berth of Canadian Pacific but they finished in the mid-1970s.

* * *

IN 1970 came word that the Mediterranean lines were proposing a consortium for containers. Manchester Liners had put on little ships to "cream the traffic" and to avoid lengthy times in port. The ML share of the West coast trade had gone down to about 5 per cent but it was a profitable 5 per cent.

Obviously, any consortium would be out of Liverpool not Manchester. Says Mr. Stoker: "We would be a very minor partner, the object of giving employment to dockers in Manchester would be negatived and furthermore, we were busy building up transhipment cargo to and from North America.

"The British lines all used the same agent in Beirut as in Israel. The rules of the game were that a vessel going to Israel could not go to an Arab country and vice-versa. So two seperate services with different vessels were run.

"We spied out the land and found in Israel a fine old-established agent, Ardo Shipping, who had been sacked by the UK lines — but our London friend asked us not to break with their new friends who represented all the British lines."

Mr Stoker and Mr D. E. Warburton, director of Manchester Prince Line, went out to sell the container concept in the broadest terms in company with a common agent.

"Then a visit was made to Cyprus", said Mr. Stoker. "It was found that Queen Victoria's regulations were still intact and the lorry with a container would need a man with a red flag in front!

"However we visited the Transport Minister and the groundwork was laid for a service there.

"When we arrived at the agent's office in Famagusta, the switchboard operator reported that the opposition agents across the road had rung up our agents asking, 'Who are the two Englishmen?'

"The Middle East is, of course, a land of mystery, so one of the visitors put on his straw hat well down over his eyes and, with dark glasses and a notebook, walked across the road into the opposition's office, making phoney notes of what he saw, into the private office of two startled partners and back across the road.

"Perhaps it was not surprising when on arrival at London airport there was a Tannoy message asking us to ring Mr Murrant, deputy chairman of Furness Withy.

"What on earth have you been doing in the Mediterranean?" he inquired.

"The next day a summit meeting was called of the top brass of the Mediterranean."

The chairman of Manchester Liners was up against the wall with the chairman and deputy chairman of Furness Withy trying to see fair play. "It was a difficult meeting with so many lawyers for the prosecution but nothing was conceded", said Mr Stoker. "The result was that we were able to say we must have our own agents.

"The scene was then shifted to a Conference meeting. One of the lines had just arranged for new conventional tonnage so was not too enthusiastic about a container service.

"Altogether there were six British lines and Zim Lines (the Israel national line) in, and our friend the Prince Line had to speak against us as they were part of the proposed new consortium from London.

"They used to have one vote but when we took over the West coast service they were reduced to half a vote — and we had half a vote. So it was 6½ votes to one against.

"We were told that we could join in at 5 per cent ex-the Mersey and our reply was that we had a ship available, the ***Manchester Merit***, which we had ordered in Spain and could start the service next month, months ahead of any other line. This was not very popular.

"On the next day we compromised and put the service off for four months to enable the lines to organise themselves.

"An uneasy peace was restored and we developed Cyprus further with a big meeting in Nicosia attended by the Transport Minister, a devotee of Shakespeare.

"Another meeting was then called in Manchester, at Manchester Liners House, hoping that our friends would be impressed by it.

"We were three times expelled from the Conference and three times brought back again, finally on the basis that we promised not to absorb any inland charges from London where the rates were much higher than from Manchester as the cargo was of better class.

"However to put pressure on us, the new Furness Withy vessel, the ***Chiltern Prince***, bound for the London consortium, was not allowed to join it, so we chartered her on our service which improved it until such time as wiser counsel prevailed and they were allowed into the London consortium.

"What is certain is that because of our dedication to the container concept we brought containers into the whole Mediterranean certainly six months before they would otherwise have taken over.

"Equally, without our strong minority interest we would have been unable to go it alone.

"It is interesting that the line which was busy building conventional vessels was the first of the main lines to give up its service."

* * *

ALSO in the Mediterranean, Furness has been trading to Greece with the old Johnston Line since the last century but they had finished their service around the end of the 1960s. The philosophy of Manchester Liners was that wherever there was no service out of Manchester to the Mediterranean the company would put ships in.

About four years later Manchester Liners put in a regular service to Greece, basically for the homeward cargo which assisted in developing the Beirut trade.

"This was a rather unpopular move with our colleagues but eventually they got used to it", said Mr Stoker.

"Other outside competitors appeared and towards the end of the decade we suggested to our principal competitor it was time we started to work together and take business from our competitors instead of from each other.

The "Manchester Merit", ordered for the Mediterranean trade.

"We made a deal with Ellermans whereby they fed traffic to us from Portugal, using our containers, and the two of us went after our competitors, one of whom folded up within the year.

"So, having been recognised as sensible, reasonable people who stood up for themselves, we became quite friendly by the end of the decade, which meant that the foundations were laid for ever closer liaison later on."

* * *

AT the time of the formation of Manchester Liners the Furness Line ships had black funnels. It was decided that Manchester Liners should have a red funnel — of a rather orangy shade — complete with a black top and a black band.

Then Christopher Furness changed the Furness Line funnel to these colours.

"Following a stormy interview with RBS, it was at once back to black," said Mr Stoker.

In 1921 Sir Frederick Lewis then changed the Furness funnels to black with a narrow and a broad red (purplish) band — and so it has been seen since in the ports of the world.

* * *

IT was around the same time that the Prince Line added the Prince of Wales feathers to the funnels of their ships.

A story about Sir James Knott, founder of the Prince Line, concerns an occasion when Knott met a group of cadets on the quayside at Newcastle and inquired, "What ship are you from, my boys?"

"The ***Sailor Prince,***" — one of the Prince Line vessels — said one of the cadets.

"Well", said Sir James, "I'm Knott".

Came the reply, "You're jolly lucky!"

* * *

SAILING in the remote and icy northern regions of Canada in the 1950s apparently involved not only the difficulties of serving rather primitive ports but also of being guided by an Eskimo pilot believed to be around 95 years of age and blind, assisted as deputy pilot by his son, a youngster of about 65.

"Legend has it that the son would say "Onk, onk, onk", meaning "There is a lone pine tree on the starboard bow", said Mr Stoker.

"Father would say "Oink", which meant "Put your wheel hard to port".

"The vessel would be steered like that for something like 34 miles!"

* * *

ANOTHER story from the period of expansion in Northern Canada concerns head salesman John Killick, who was in the United States city of Savannah, Georgia, and complaining about the heat. He was sent to the cold far North — to Churchill, on Hudson's Bay, joining colleague Harry Harrison, who was awaiting the arrival of the next Manchester Liners ship.

Says Mr Stoker: "Harrison, later to become manager in Vancouver, is the man who, after six weeks in Churchill, earned immortality by sending his boss a postcard picture of an Eskimo woman smoking a pipe. Wrote Harrison, 'She is starting to look attractive. Please can I come home?"

* * *

DURING the unofficial strike of seamen in 1960, directed more at officers of the union than the shipowners, the wives of strikers were given a breakdown of earnings of their husbands. It was not a popular move in some quarters.

In an effort to keep matters good-humoured, Mr Stoker offered a "Kentucky breakfast" to any seaman who had received less than a certain figure on a voyage.

A "Kentucky breakfast" is a bottle of whisky and a steak — you give the steak to the dog!

An argument developed over whether "Sundays at sea money" should be included. Compromising, Mr Stoker presented a bottle of rum, which was promptly raffled by the unofficial strike committee as "the management's personal contribution to the strike fund!"

On hearing of this ingenuity, Mr Stoker commented, "Thank goodness I didn't offer 200 bottles of whisky!"

* * *

FOR some years after the First World War Manchester Liners had carried up to 12 passengers in the cargo vessels, this ending after the Second World War as passenger airliners began to take over.

On onc passenger voyage, the master, Cape Horner Capt Foale, had been told to be specially polite to an important guest, a lady who while dining could not get the salt out of the salt cellar. Gallantly, the captain said, "Let me help you, madam". He picked up the salt cellar and blew down its top!

* * *

WHEN the ***Manchester Shipper*** and ***Manchester Pioneer*** were chosen to star in the film of Shelagh Delaney's novel "A Taste of Honey", it was not known that part of the plot involved a drunken seaman taking his girl friend on board, involving an also drunken chief officer!

When the premiere took place, the company had to take space in the programme to point out that Manchester Liners neither approved nor allowed such conduct!

* * *

THE company was, of course, learning about container handling when the ***Manchester Shipper*** was fitted with a derrick crane for the pilot scheme between Manchester and Chicago.

In Chicago the port labour seemed to delight in seeing how big a hole they could make in the containers with fork-lift trucks. Another problem was controlling the movement of containers. In Manchester there was a ticket for each container giving a number and routing directions hooked on to a destination dividing board.

Nobody visualised how vigorously these would be dusted by the dusting ladies. Much time was spent picking up the labels from the floor so a better system was devised.

* * *

WHISKY was one of the most vulnerable conventionally-shipped cargoes. Cases were easily opened, bottles taken and bricks of the right weight substituted. A case dropped on its corner would enable a bowler hat to be filled.

A St John legend is that some people, knowing the exact spot in the shed where the whisky would be stowed, would go out on Sundays in a boat complete with a bath-tub, rowing underneath the shed.

As the tide lifted the boat to the underside of the floor they would drill with an awl through the wooden timbers and into the barrel, filling the bath-tub.

The change to containers certainly cut pilferage.

* * *

DURING a visit to Canada, the Russian leader Kosygin expressed a wish to see the Manchester Liners Container Terminal at Montreal. Mr P. V. O. Evans and Mr Stoker — who was carrying a shooting stick and wearing a Sherlock Holmes hat — went there to meet him.

A posse of police arrived on motor cycles, then a car with the flag of the lilies of Quebec, out of which stepped Port Manager Monsieur Guy Beaudet,

Seen loading at the Manchester Container Terminal is the "Manchester Concept".

followed by a car bearing a hammer and sickle motif, carrying Mr Kosygin and his aides.

M. Beaudet and Mr Stoker exchanged cordial greeting. Mr Kosygin pointed at Mr Stoker and said, with some disfavour: "That is an Englishman?" "Yes," said M. Beaudet.

"But you seem very friendly with him", said Mr Kosygin. "Well, he's a nice chap", said M. Beaudet.

My Kosygin then said: "Yes, but what is he doing here?" M. Beaudet replied: "He runs the ships up here."

"Do you charge him less than you charge me?" asked Mr Kosygin.

Mr Stoker felt he really ought to intervene so he said, "Now, Mr Kosygin, you see all those containers stacked up there? I painted them red especially for you. And you might like to know that our strong ice-strengthened vessels come up the St Lawrence breaking the ice for yours that come along behind — and we don't charge you anything."

Mr Kosygin immediately burst out laughing.

This, at first, seemed puzzling as all the conversation was being translated by an interpreter into Russian. However it transpired that Mr Kosygin had started his working life as an apprentice with Platt Brothers in Oldham, Lancashire, and knew English perfectly!

The party then became quite informal and friendly.

As a tailpiece to this story, Mr Stoker was in Greece some time later when he was invited on board a Russian cruise ship as guest of the head of the Russian Merchant Marine, to whom he said, "By the way, I was talking to your boss the other day."

"But I haven't got a boss", the Russian replied.

Mr Stoker explained that he was referring to a "chap called Kosygin", to which the reply was, "Oh, you mean God!"

Evidently, Russia is not entirely an atheist country.

* * *

Fleet List

Name	Gross tons	Built	Disposal
Manchester Enterprise (ex-***Queensmore***)	3,878	1890	Bought from E. D. and Co. Ltd. Foundered 50 deg. 25 min. N., 42 deg. 25 min. W., on passage Manchester-Montreal, November 15, 1899.
Manchester Trader (ex-***Parkmore***)	3,318	1890	Bought from E. D. and Co. Ltd. Sold 1913 and renamed ***Ferdinand Melsom***. Resold 1915 to Westfal Larsen (Norway) and renamed ***Kaupanger***. Torpedoed in the Mediterranean December 13, 1916.
Manchester City	7,696	1898	Broken up June 1929 by Stavanger Shipbreaking Company, Norway (one time biggest meat ship).
Manchester Port	5,658	1899	Sold to R. P. Houston and Company, and renamed ***Hydaspes*** in 1900. broken up in Italy, 1930.
Manchester Merchant	5,657	1900	Scuttled on fire Dingle Bay, January 15, 1903 on passage New Orleans-Manchester.
Manchester Corporation	5,400	1899	Scrapped July 1929 by T. W. Ward, at Barrow.
Manchester Commerce	5,363	1899	Mined off Tory Island, October 27, 1914.
Manchester Importer	4,028	1899	Sold to Greeks in 1927 as the ***Alexandria***. Scrapped in 1933 at Venice.
Manchester Shipper	4,038	1900	Sold and broken up in July 1930 by T. W. Ward, at Briton Ferry.
Manchester Exchange	4,091	1901	Delivered November 16, 1901. Sold in 1925 to Finland as the ***Equator***. Sold for scrap 1939 to Italy.
Manchester Engineer	4,302	1902	Delivered on February 25, 1902. Torpedoed March 27, 1916, West of Coningbeg lightvessel.
Manchester Inventor	4,247	1902	Delivered on April 8, 1902. Torpedoed off the Fastnet, January 18, 1917.
Manchester Market	4,901	1902	Delivered on January 23, 1902. Wrecked April 26, 1903 near Tuskar Rock on passage Manchester-Philadelphia.
Manchester Spinner	4,227	1903	Delivered on July 11, 1903 and torpedoed South of Malta on January 22, 1918.
Manchester Miller	4,234	1903	Delivered August 22, 1903. Long Time Charter to Watts, Watts and Company and renamed ***Fulham*** in 1905. Back to Manchester Liners in 1908 as ***Manchester Miller***. Torpedoed on June 5, 1917, 190 miles N.W. of the Fastnet.
Manchester Merchant	4,152	1904	Delivered on January 14, 1904. Sold for breaking up in October 1933.
Manchester Port	4,093	1904	Delivered January 11, 1904. Sold in 1925 to H. Vogemann, Hamburg and renamed ***Vogesen***. Mined off Vinga May 7, 1940.
Manchester Mariner	4,106	1904	Delivered on January 28, 1904. Mined in English Channel December 4, 1917, but towed in. Sold in 1925 to Finland; became ***Mercator***. Mined and sunk S.E. of Buchan Ness, December 1, 1939.
Manchester Citizen	4,251	1912	Delivered on June 18, 1912. Torpedoed April 26, 1917, N.W. of the Fastnet.
Manchester Civilian	4,706	1913	Delivered August 28, 1913. Sold to Greece as ***Tasis*** in 1933. Taken by Vichy France at Dakar in June 1940 and renamed ***Equateur***. Taken over by Italy in 1942 and renamed ***Bari***. Lost by air attack at Naples on August 1, 1943.
Manchester Hero	5,738	1916	Sold in 1937 to B. and N. Shipping Company, and renamed ***St. Winifred***. Sold to Italy in 1939 as ***Capo Vita***. Torpedoed west of Lampedusa Island March 9, 1941 by British submarine.
Manchester Trader (ex-***Archenbloe***)	3,938	1902	Purchased from Purdie, Glen and Company, Glasgow in 1916. Sunk by submarine gunfire, June 4, 1917, in the Mediterranean, off Pantellaria.
Manchester Engineer (ex-***Nation***, ex-***Craigvar***)	4,415	1905	Purchased in 1917 from W. Thaner and Company, Liverpool, for the one lost above in this year. Torpedoed August 16, 1917, North Sea off Flamborough Head.
Manchester Inventor (ex-***Celtic King***)	4,112	1907	Sunk by submarine gunfire in North Sea, N.E. of Muckle Flugga, on July 30, 1917.
Manchester Commerce (ex-***King***)	4,144	1906	Purchased about 1916. Torpedoed N.W. of Cape Spartel, June 29, 1917.
Manchester Brigade	6,021	1918	Delivered on July 30, 1918. Torpedoed West of Malin Head, September 26, 1940.

Name	Gross tons	Built	Disposal
Manchester Division	6,027	1918	Delivered on September 28, 1918. Scrapped December 2, 1953 arrived at Briton Ferry for T. W. Ward.
Manchester Producer (ex-***Start Point***)	6,576	1916	Purchased from Furness, Withy, April 3, 1921. Sold 1939 Botwey (Board of Trade). Torpedoed N.W. of St. Kilda, July 26, 1941.
Manchester Spinner (ex-***Grampian Range***)	4,767	1918	Purchased from Furness, Withy, April 4, 1921. Sunk Normandy Beaches as blockship for Mulberry Harbour, June 9, 1944.
Manchester Regiment	7,930	1922	Launched Tees September 15, 1922. Lost in convoy collision with steamer ***Oropesa***, S.W. of Cape Race, December 4, 1939.
Manchester Commerce	5,342	1925	Delivered July 26, 1923. Sold to Camel Lines January 1952 and renamed ***Corbita***. resold 1952 to East and West Steamship Co., Karachi. Renamed ***Fakirjee Cowasjee***. Broken up at Karachi 1967.
Manchester Citizen	5,328	1925	Delivered August 26, 1925. Torpedoed and sunk S.E. of Accra on July 9, 1943.
Manchester Exporter (ex-***Rexmore***)	5,277	1918	Purchased from Johnston Line (Furness, Withy), October 20, 1929. Sold 1947 to Lambert Bros. as ***Nicaragua*** (Panama flag). To China in 1948 as ***Yu Tung***, and in 1950 to Wallem and Company, Panama, as the ***Rio Bamba***. Renamed in 1952 ***Precila***. Broken up in Japan 1958.
El Argentino	9,501	1928	Acquired half interest. Sold in 1937. Sunk by air attack N.W. of Lisbon on July 26, 1943.
Manchester Port	5,649	1935	Delivered October 7, 1935. 1964: Sold to Spanish shipbreakers.
Manchester City	5,600	1937	H.M.S. in World War II. 1964: Sold to Shipbreaking Industries Ltd., Faslane.
Manchester Progress	5,620	1938	Delivered September 17, 1938. 1966: Sold to Brodospas, Split, Yugoslavia for breaking up.
Manchester Merchant	7,264	1940	Delivered May 18, 1940. Torpedoed February 25, 1943, East of Cape Race.
Manchester Trader	5,670	1941	Delivered May 30, 1941. 1963: Sold to Brodospas, Split, Yugoslavia for breaking up.
Manchester Shipper	7,881	1943	Delivered October, 10, 1943. 1969: Sold to Italian shipbreakers at Trieste.
Manchester Regiment	5,825	1947	Delivered February, 27, 1947. 1968: Sold to Panamanian flag owners; renamed ***Azure Coast II***. 1971: Sold to Singapore owners; renamed ***Pu gor***. 1971: Broken up in Taiwan.
Manchester Merchant	7,651	1951	Delivered January 18, 1951. 1967: Sold to Liberian flag owners; renamed ***Clio***. 14.2.1972: Sank after fire on passage Chittagong to Continent.
Manchester Pioneer	1,805	1952	Delivered April 2, 1952. 2.1960: Lengthened by Manchester Dry Docks from 250 ft. to 290 ft. 1963: Sold to Greek buyers; renamed ***Cyprian Med***. 1970: Renamed ***Agios Antonios***.
Manchester Explorer	1,805	1952	Delivered May 15, 1952. 1963: Sold to Crosbie Shipping Co., Canada; renamed ***C. A. Crosbie***. 1965: renamed ***P. M. Crosbie***. 1968: Sold to Pamagos Shipping Co., Cyprus; renamed ***Panegious***. 1971: renamed ***Ypermachos***.
Manchester Spinner	7,814	1952	Delivered July 4, 1952. 1968: Sold to Estia Cia. Nav. S.A., Panama; renamed ***Estia***. Sank after engine room explosion.
Manchester Prospector	1,400	1948	1953: Bought from S. Ugelstad, Oslo; ex-***Vigor***. 1960: Sold to Chr. M. Salvis and Co., Greece; renamed ***Georgios***. 1973: Sold to "Lassa" Special Shipping S.A., Patras; renamed ***Aghios Nektarios L***.
Manchester Mariner	7,580	1955	Delivered March 3, 1955. 1968: Sold to Mira Cia. Nav. S.A., Panama; renamed ***Ira***.
Manchester Vanguard	1,662	1956	Delivered April 19, 1956. 1963: Sold to General Steam Navigation Co., London; renamed ***Sheldrake***. 1968: Sold to Israeli flag owners, renamed ***Bat Golan***. 1974: To Panamanian flag; renamed ***Woodchuck***. 1975: To Singapore flag; renamed ***Selatan Maru***. First vessel into St. Lawrence Seaway 1959.

Name	Gross tons	Built	Disposal
Manchester Venture	1,662	1956	1961: Sold to General Steam Navigation Co. Ltd., London; renamed ***Philomel***. 1968: sold to Israeli flag owners; renamed ***Bat Tiran***. 8.1972: Beached at Piraeus after explosion and fire. Broken up.
Manchester Faith	4,459	1959	1965: Chartered to Cairn Line, renamed ***Cairnesk***. 1967: Reverted to ***Manchester Faith***. 1970: Sold to Alimos Shipping Co., Panama; renamed ***Ilkon Tak***.
Manchester Fame	4,462	1959	1965: Chartered to Cairn Line Ltd., Newcastle; renamed ***Cairnglen***. 1966: Reverted to ***Cairnglen***. 1970: Sold to Kalamaki Shipping and Trading Co., Panama; renamed ***Ilkon Niki***.
Manchester Miller	9,296	1959	1970: Converted to cellular container ship by Smith's Dock Co. Ltd., South Bank on Tees; renamed ***Manchester Quest***. 1976: Sold to Mitsui Co., Japan. Re-sold to Taiwan shipbreakers.
Manchester Trader (chartered vessel)	5,758	1955	1963: Chartered from Prince Line Ltd., London; ex-***Western Prince***. Re-delivered to Prince Line 13.1.69 and reverted to ***Western Prince***.
Manchester Commerce	8,724	1963	1971: Sold to W. L. Suan, Hong Kong; renamed ***Ber Sea***. 1975: Sold to People's Republic of China; renamed ***Yangchun***. 1980: Gutted by fire following shelling in the Shatt el Arab, Khorramshahr.
Manchester City	8,734	1964	1971: Sold to Korea Shipping Corporation; renamed ***Korean Winner***. 1978: Sold to Yin Tang Shipping Co. Ltd., Seoul; renamed ***One West No. 8***.
Manchester Renown	8,742	1964	1971: Sold to Korea Shipping Corporation; renamed ***Korean Challenger***. 1978: Sold to Whitney Shipping Co., Monrovia; renamed ***Edessa*** (Greek flag).
Manchester Freighter	8,105	1959	1965: Taken over from Cairn Line Ltd.; ex-***Cairnforth***. 1969: Sold to Royal Mail Lines Ltd., London; renamed ***Lombardy***.
Manchester Exporter	7,506	1952	1965: Taken over from Cairn Line Ltd.; ex-***Cairndhu***. 1969: Sold to Greek buyers.
Manchester Engineer	7,503	1952	1965: Taken over from Cairn Line Ltd.; ex-***Cairngowan***. 1966: Reverted to Cairn Line as ***Cairngowan***. 1969: Sold to Mananto Shipping Co., Famagusta; renamed ***Georgilos***.
Manchester Port	8,938	1966	1971: Sold to Yugoslav buyers; renamed ***Biokovo***.
Manchester Progress	8,176	1967	1971: Converted to cellular container ship at Amsterdam; renamed ***Manchester Concept***. 1973: sold to Mercantile Leasing Co. ltd., London, remaining under Manchester Liners management. 1980: Sold to Singapore flag owners; renamed ***Cherry Bunga***.
Manchester Challenge (cc)	12,039	1968	1979: Sold to Hong Kong Ocean Shipping Co. Ltd., Monrovia; renamed ***Ocean Container*** (Panamanian flag).
Manchester Courage (cc)	12,039	1968	1979: Sold to Carolina Leasing Ltd., London, who demise chartered her to Hong Kong Island Shipping Co., Monrovia; renamed ***Pacific Container***.
Manchester Concorde (cc)	12,039	1969	1982: Sold to Char Lian Marine (Panama) S.A.; renamed ***Char Lian***. 1.1984: Broken up.
Manchester Merit (cc)	3,414	1970	1970: Acquired from Baasa-Salubre S.A., Santander; launched as ***Catalina del Mar***; renamed ***Manchester Merito***. 1970: Renamed ***Manchester Merit***. 1972: Demise chartered to Plumbton Shipping Corporation, Bermuda; renamed ***Fortuna***. 1975: Sold to Chelwood Shipping Co., Monrovia; renamed ***Kathleen***.
Manchester Crusade (cc)	12,039	1971	1982: Sold to Char Lian Marine, Taiwan; renamed ***Char Che***. 1.1984: Broken up.
Manchester Frontier (cc) (chartered vessel)	3,621	1972	1972: Bought from shipbuilders, Astilleros del Atlantico, Santander by Condron (Manchester) Ltd. and chartered to Manchester Liners Ltd.; ex-***Frontier***. Later bought by Manchester Liners (Freighting) Ltd. and charter continued. 1979: Sold to Bayworth Shipping Corporation, Monrovia; renamed ***Box Trader*** (Greek Flag). 1984: Sold to Wex Ford Shipping Co., Limassol; renamed ***Haris***.

Name	Gross tons	Built	Disposal
Manchester Vigour (cc)	5,310	1973	1980: Sold to Compagnie Maritime d'Affretement, Marseilles; renamed ***Ville d'Orient***.
Manchester Zeal (cc)	5,310	1973	1981: Sold to Pacific International Lines (Pte.) Ltd., Singapore; renamed ***Sea Hawk***.
Manchester Renown (cc)	12,577	1974	1974: Chartered to China Navigation Co.; renamed ***Asian Renown***. 1978: Reverted to ***Manchester Renown***. 1982: Sold to Karana Line, Jakarta; renamed ***R. R. Ratih***.
Manchester Reward (cc)	12,577	1974	1974: Chartered to China Navigation Co.; renamed ***Asian Reward***. 1978: Reverted to ***Manchester Reward***. 1982: Sold to Famous Steamship S.A., Monrovia; renamed ***R. S. Ratna***.
Manchester Falcon (cc) (chartered vessel)	999	1975	1975: Chartered from Partenreederei m.s. "Lappland", Rendsburg, as ***Lappland***; renamed ***Manchester Falcon***. 1976: Re-delivered to owners; reverted to ***Lappland***.
Manchester Vanguard (cc)	17,385	1977	Owners: Golden Cross Line Ltd., demise chartered to Manchester Liners. 1977: Chartered to Seatrain Lines; renamed ***Seatrain Trenton***. 1978: reverted to ***Manchester Vanguard***. 1979: Chartered to Gold Star Line, Hong Kong; renamed ***Keelung***. 1980: Reverted to ***Manchester Vanguard***. 1980: Chartered to C. Y. Tung group; renamed ***Oriental Vanguard***. 1981: Reverted to ***Manchester Vanguard***. 1982: Chartered to United Arab Shipping Co.; renamed ***Ibn Majid***. 1983: Sold to C. Y. Tung group; renamed ***Oriental Expert*** (now Taiwanese flag).
Manchester Venture (cc)	17,385	1977	Owners: Gough and Crosthwaite, demise chartered to Manchester Liners. 1977: Chartered to Seatrain Lines; renamed ***Seatrain Bennington***. 1978: Reverted to ***Manchester Venture***. 1979: Chartered to Gold Star Line, Hong Kong; renamed ***Marseille***. 1980: Reverted to ***Manchester Venture***. 1980: Chartered to C. Y. Tung group; renamed ***Oriental Venture***. 1981: Chartered to Hapag-Lloyd; renamed ***Rhein Express***. 1983: To C. Y. Tung group; renamed ***Oriental Venture***. 1984: Renamed ***Oriental Ambassador*** (Island Navigation Corporation (Ship Management) Ltd., Hong Kong.
Lindo (cc) (chartered vessel)	6,411	1972	1973: Chartered for Great Lakes feeder service. Owners: Reederei D. Oltmann KG, Bremen.
Manchester Faith (cc) (chartered vessel)	1,421	1974	1974: Chartered from Walter Bartels, Hamburg. 1983: Re-delivered to owner; renamed ***Francop***.
Manchester Mercurio (cc) (chartered vessel)	1,997	1971	1971: Chartered from Naviera Santa Catalina S.A., Gijon. 1980: Re-delivered to owner.
Manchester Rapido (cc) (chartered vessel)	1,997	1971	1971: Launched as ***Esther del Mar*** for Equimar Maritima S.A., Bilbao. 1971: Chartered by Manchester Liners Ltd.; renamed ***Manchester Rapido***. 1978: Re-delivered to owner; reverted to ***Esther del Mar***.
Manchester Shipper (chartered vessel)	500	1973	1974: Chartered from Knud Danielsen Partrederi, Copenhagen, as ***Peter Theilgaard***. Renamed ***Manchester Shipper***. 1975: Re-delivered to owner; reverted to ***Peter Theilgaard***.
Manchester Fulmar (cc) (chartered vessel)	2,524	1974	1974: Chartered from Maritima Astur S.A., Gijon, as ***Fulmar***. 1975: Renamed ***Manchester Fulmar***. 1979: Re-delivered to owners; reverted to ***Fulmar***.
Manchester Clipper (cc) (chartered vessel)	1,595	1980	1980: Chartered from Harald Winter, Hamburg, ex-***Clipper***. 1983: Re-delivered to owner; renamed ***Clipper***.
Manchester Eagle (cc) (chartered vessel)	965	1972	1981: Chartered from Gerhard Schepers, Papenburg; ex-***Atlantic Eagle***. 1982: Re-delivered to owner; renamed ***Eagle*** (Singapore flag).
Manchester Fulmar (cc) (chartered vessel)	1,599	1979	1981: Chartered from Ellerman City Liners, as ***City of Ipswich***; renamed ***Manchester Fulmar***. 1983: Re-delivered to owners; reverted to ***City of Ipswich***.
Manchester Crown (cc)	1,599	1979	1983: Transferred from Prince Line; ex-***Crown Prince***. 1985: Sold to Thai Overseas Lines; renamed ***Thai Amber***.

Name	*Gross tons*	*Built*	*Disposal*
Manchester Trader (cc) (chartered vessel)	1,999	1977	1984: Chartered from Gerhard Schepers, Papenburg; ex-***Lamara*** Singapore flag. 1985: Re-delivered to owners; reverted to ***Lamara***.

SHIPS OPERATING 1981-

Manchester Challenge (cc)	30,817	1970	1981: Transferred from Dart Container Line; ex-***Dart America***.
Manchester Faith (CC) (chartered vessel)	1,599	1971	1985: Chartered from Helmut Bastian, Bremen, as ***Nahorst Kurier***. Renamed ***Manchester Faith***.
Manchester City (cc) (chartered vessel)	3,598	1978	1985: Chartered from Johs. Thade, Hamburg, as ***City of Lisbon***, under which name she had been chartered to Ellerman City Liners; renamed ***Manchester City***.
Manchester Trader (cc) (chartered vessel)	3,978	1978	1985: Chartered from Helmut Bastian, Bremen, as ***Kormoran***. Renamed ***Manchester Trader***.

(cc) = cellular container ship

WORLD SHIP SOCIETY

Founded in 1947, the World Ship Society has extensive documentary and photographic records of ships, present and past. It has published the fleet histories of numerous companies including, in 1985, Bank Line and Blue Star Line. The Society's monthly magazine ''Marine News'' gives information about launchings, sales, losses and scrappings. For full details and sample magazine send 20p in stamps to: WSS, 58 Bicton Street, Exmouth, Devon.

MERSEYSIDE MARITIME MUSEUM

Merseyside Maritime Museum, adjacent to Liverpool's Pier Head, encompasses historic docks and buildings with wide-ranging displays on the history of the great port of Liverpool and its ships and sailors. It includes working exhibits on boat-building, model-making and coopering, together with the Piermaster's House. Full-size vessels include the pilot boat ***Edmund Gardner***, the schooner ***De Wadden*** and Sir Alec Rose's ***Lively Lady***. An exhibition opening Spring 1986 entitled ''Emigrants to the New World'' is about the nine million people who left Liverpool between 1830 and 1930 in search of a better life.

THE BOAT MUSEUM

This National Waterways Museum at Ellesmere Port, Cheshire, is listed as one of the top ten attractions in the North West. A working museum, it has over 50 historic canal and estuarial craft. Within this unique dock complex are indoor exhibitions on canals, the local town and energy. There are regular boat trips, a well-stocked shop, a cafe and a picnic area. The museum transports visitors back into the life and times of the canal age, which helped to start the Industrial Revolution in Britain. The Boat Museum was winner of the Council of Europe's Museum of the Year Award in 1984, is Britain's premier canal museum.

EXETER MARITIME MUSEUM

Exeter Maritime Museum contains the largest collection of ethnic working boats in the world with some afloat that can be boarded and others in warehouses. The Museum sails quite a number of these boats. A visitor to Manchester along the Manchester Ship Canal in the early 1980s from the Museum was the 60-foot Chinese junk ***Keying II***. The Museum is at The Quay, Exeter.

THE GREATER MANCHESTER MUSEUM OF SCIENCE AND INDUSTRY

The world's oldest railway station, in Liverpool Road, is the home of this new Museum at Castlefield, Manchester, an area which is a tourist ''must''. The Museum contains many fine examples of the products of the industrially important North West region. There is a strong emphasis on working exhibits including steam mill engines which are demonstrated every afternoon. There is an air and space gallery, an electricity gallery and a workshop in which visitors can watch craftsmen restoring machines.